the ART of the cookie

RECIPES Shelly Kaldunski

PHOTOGRAPHS Maren Caruso

weldonowen

CONTENTS

MODERN CLASSICS

ALL ABOUT CREATIVE COOKIES

There are cookies, and then there are *special* cookies. These are the cookies that you press into festive shapes, pipe frosting onto with artistic flair, or cover in colored sugar crystals, as you may have done when you were little. The child in every home baker still enjoys exploring the many ways that cookies can be made into little works of edible art.

In these pages, you'll find recipes and ideas that will help you tap into your creative side, inspiring you to craft cookies that delight the senses well before they are devoured. The book begins with five basic cookie recipes featuring different flavors: vanilla, lemon-buttermilk, brown sugar, chocolate, and gingerbread. These favorites become the canvas for a wealth of decorating ideas: brightly hued flowers sprinkled with sanding sugar, colorful squares inspired by the designs on ceramic tiles, and circles adorned with whimsical polka dots of various shades and sizes. Next come recipes for classic cookies that take on a modern twist. Chewy oatmeal lace drizzled in chocolate and caramel, shiny meringue piped into spirals, and elegant vanilla spritz made into sandwiches with a chocolate center are just a few of the offerings.

Confections this lovely and delicious beg to be shared. Present them on an elegant platter or cake stand for a welcome contribution to any event, whether it's a winter holiday party, an open house, Mother's Day tea, or a cookie exchange (page 8), or tuck them away in a care package for your favorite college student or a friend in need. With such gorgeous offerings, your friends and family may protest that you've gone to too much trouble, but the truth is that cookie decorating is easily doable with the help of a few basic kitchen tools and ingredients, along with some handy how-to's and illustrated techniques, all covered here.

COOKIES AS ART

The recipes, decorating ideas, and tips in these pages are designed both to inspire you and to show that you don't need a painter's hand or endless hours to create stunning cookies. Even the more ornate creations should not be intimidating—the recipes will guide you step-by-step through the process and the more complicated recipes come with illustrations that highlight specific techniques. Don't be surprised if you find yourself coming up with your own ideas on how to shape, ice, adorn, and package your cookies. Remember to have fun, and the decorating will come easily.

GIVE A LITTLE, GET A LITTLE

HOSTING A COOKIE EXCHANGE An exciting way to share, and maybe even show off, your eye-catching creations is through a cookie exchange party. Guests bring their favorite homemade cookies to display and exchange, and each person at the party goes home with samples and recipes. Cookie exchanges are a winter holiday party classic, and they also make enjoyable activities for other occasions such as birthdays, brunches, and showers.

A cookie exchange party has all of the makings and charm of a potluck—and is as easy to host. Two to three weeks before the date of your get-together, send invitations or an e-mail with the basic information: time, place, and an RSVP request. Since a cookie exchange might be new for some guests, briefly explain in the invitation that each guest should bring one to two dozen cookies to sample and exchange, along with enough copies of the recipe to share.

Let guests know that this is a chance to sample and talk about a wide range of recipes, whether new or familiar. You can let your guests choose a type of cookie, or you can suggest a theme, such as flowers for an outdoor garden party, goblins and ghouls for Halloween, or a winter wonderland of stars and trees for Christmas.

Depending on the occasion and time of day, consider offering a few savory snacks and appropriate beverages, such as coffee, tea, sparkling water, or wine. On the day of the cookie exchange, set up a table that can accommodate everyone's offerings, and have ready jars, boxes, bags, or colorful papers and string that guests can use to take cookies home.

THE COOKIE ARTIST'S TOOLKIT

Like artists, cookie crafters like to stock an array of supplies. Look for these supplies in a supermarket or specialty kitchen shop, or purchase them online.

COCONUT Sweetened, toasted, or dried, shreds and flakes of coconut contribute texture, shape, and flavor to cookies as a topping or as an ingredient.

DARK CHOCOLATE PEARLS Pearls, as the name indicates, are round confections rather than shaped like the candies sold as chocolate chips. Common sizes are ¼ inch (6 mm) and ½ inch (12 mm).

DRAGÉES These tiny beads, often used sparingly as an accent, add glamour to any cookie. They are commonly available in silver and gold. Made of sugar, they have a coating that contains a trace amount of metal. Although dragées are considered nontoxic, the U.S. Food and Drug Administration recommends removing them before serving.

FOOD COLORING Dyes of various colors and forms (liquid, powder, and gel-paste) are used to tint icings and frostings. Gel-paste food colorings come in a wider array of colors and are preferable to other forms of food coloring because they blend easier. A small amount of food coloring goes a long way, so be sure to start with just a drop or two to mix in before adding more.

JIMMIES These small candies come in colors from orange and yellow to a mixture of hues in a single package. White and milk chocolate jimmies are the classic versions.

LUSTER DUST Adding a metallic sheen to decorations, luster dust is a powder that is mixed with a flavoring extract and then applied with a clean, small paintbrush. The most common colors are silver and gold. Other colors, from subtle to bright, are also available.

NONPAREILS With the help of tweezers, these tiny beads of sugar can be arranged on iced cookies to make an infinite number of designs. They are available in a rainbow of colors.

NUTS Nearly all nuts—almonds, pecans, pistachios, walnuts—add flavor and texture to cookies. They are often toasted beforehand to bring out their distinctive flavor and character before being used in dough or as decoration.

SANDING SUGAR Perhaps the simplest of all decorating supplies are colored sugar crystals. Their chunky, unrefined form reflects light. They are the perfect choice when you want translucent, unsaturated colors and confections that sparkle.

COOKIE BAKER'S EQUIPMENT

Take stock of your kitchen. For making cookies, you'll want to have mixing bowls of various sizes, dry and liquid measuring cups, measuring spoons, wooden spoons, a rolling pin, baking sheets, and an electric mixer. Here are some other pieces of equipment that are invaluable for baking. Most can be found in a specialty kitchen shop or can be ordered online.

COOKIE CUTTERS Start out with a collection of round metal cookies cutters in various diameters. Then, depending on the recipe, you'll want to acquire cutters in squares, rectangles, stars, trees, and even more fanciful shapes. Metal cutters ensure that cookies have clean edges.

OFFSET SPATULA A metal offset spatula, with an angle in the blade, is the best tool for spreading icing or jam on cookies. These spatulas come in a variety of sizes, so find one with a blade about 4 inches (10 cm) long. The spatula should not exceed about 8 inches (20 cm) total.

PARCHMENT PAPER Lining a baking sheet with parchment paper allows for easy removal of baked cookies and the sheets generally do not need to be greased because the paper protects the bottoms of the cookies from scorching. Parchment paper is also used for making paper cones for piping (page 15).

PASTRY BAG AND TIPS A number of recipes in this book call for piping icing on cookies (page 15), and some require multiple bags and tips for two or three colors of icing. Bags come with a collection of plain and fluted tips and often with tips for creating other piped designs. Before you decorate cookies, you can practice by piping icing on a clean plate.

SMALL PAINTBRUSHES For detailed work, like painting crosshatch marks or brushing with luster dust, paintbrushes are indispensable. Buy new brushes in different sizes. Wash them in cold water and a little soap between uses, let them air dry.

SILICONE BAKING MATS These flexible, nonstick, heat-resistant mats are used to line baking sheets. They alleviate the need to grease the pan and are especially handy for delicate cookies.

TOOTHPICKS Adding food coloring to white royal icing has to be done carefully and with very tiny amounts. A toothpick is helpful for this as it is for testing cakelike cookies for doneness.

WIRE RACKS The most efficient way to cool cookies before decorating is to transfer them from the baking sheets to wire racks. This allows for air circulation and prevents them from baking further due to the residual heat on the baking sheets.

WORKING WITH A PAPER CONE

Piping may seem intimidating at first, but it becomes easier with practice. When piping icing or glazes onto cookies, a paper cone made from parchment paper is easy to use because it holds a smaller amount of icing, which is all that is needed for cookies; they are also easier to make and fill when several different colors of icing are needed. Paper cones are disposable, making cleanup easier.

1. Start with a large triangular piece of parchment paper. With the center point of the triangle facing you, make the cone's tip by placing your index finger in the middle of the base, and roll one of the side points toward the center.

2. Continue rolling the paper to form a cone, keeping its tip as tight as possible. Use your fingers to guide and secure the tip.

3. Adjust the tightness at the tip of the cone by pulling on the ends of the paper, then fold the ends inside the cone to secure it.

4. To fill the cone, hold it open with one hand and, using a teaspoon, fill it about three-fourths full with icing or whatever you will be decorating with. Once the cone is filled, fold the ends of the paper over a few times to keep the icing from leaking out. Snip a small bit off the end (or as directed in the recipe) of the cone to begin piping.

USING A PASTRY BAG

To use a pastry bag, first fit the tip into the bag by pushing it down into the small hole in the bag.

Next, form a cuff by folding down the top of the bag to one-third of its length.

Place one hand under the cuff. Use a silicone spatula to scoop the filling into the large opening in the bag, filling it no more than half full. Unfold the cuff and push the filling down toward the tip, forcing out any air bubbles. Keep the mixture flowing steadily by twisting the bag at the location where the filling ends.

With your dominant hand, hold the bag at the twist. With your non-dominant hand, hold the bag near the tip and proceed to pipe.

DECORATED FAVORITES

Buttery and crisp, these sugar cookies have a delicate vanilla flavor that makes them delicious on their own. Transformed with icing and sprinkles, they become even more appealing and festive.

3 cups (15 oz/470 g) all-purpose flour, plus more for dusting

1 teaspoon baking powder

½ teaspoon salt

1 cup (8 oz/250 g) unsalted butter, at room temperature

1¼ cups (10 oz/315 g) sugar

1 large egg

2 teaspoons pure vanilla extract

1 tablespoon heavy cream

VANILLA SUGAR COOKIES
makes about 30 cookies

1   In a bowl, whisk together the 3 cups flour, baking powder, and salt. In a large bowl, using an electric mixer on medium-high speed, beat the butter and sugar until light and fluffy, 2–3 minutes. Add the egg and vanilla and beat on low speed until the egg is completely incorporated. Beating on low speed, slowly add the flour mixture and continue to beat until almost incorporated. Add the cream and beat on low speed until just incorporated, scraping down the sides of the bowl as needed.

2   Press the dough into a rough rectangle, wrap tightly in plastic wrap, and refrigerate until firm, at least 1 hour or up to overnight. (The dough can be wrapped well and frozen for up to 1 month.)

3   Follow the desired recipe for rolling and cutting, or do the following: Preheat the oven to 350°F (180°C). Line 3 baking sheets with parchment paper. On a lightly floured work surface, using a floured rolling pin, roll out the chilled dough until about ¼ inch (6 mm) thick. Using cookie cutters or a paring knife, cut the cookies into the desired shapes. Use a metal spatula to transfer the cookies to the prepared sheets, spacing them 1 inch (2.5 cm) apart. Press the dough scraps together, roll out, and cut out additional shapes.

4   Follow the desired recipe for baking and cooling or do the following: Bake 1 sheet at a time until the cookies are lightly golden around the edges but the tops are barely colored, 16–19 minutes (or as indicated in the recipe). Let cool on the sheets for 5 minutes. Using the metal spatula, transfer to wire racks and let cool completely, about 30 minutes.

5   Decorate the cookies as desired.

For an extra-crisp and refreshing treat, brush the cutout shapes with I tablespoon buttermilk and sprinkle with sanding sugar before baking the cookies.

LEMON-BUTTERMILK COOKIES
makes about 24 cookies

3 cups (15 oz/470 g) all-purpose flour, plus more for dusting

¾ teaspoon baking soda

½ teaspoon cream of tartar

¼ teaspoon salt

¾ cup (6 oz/185 g) unsalted butter, at room temperature

1 cup (8 oz/250 g) granulated sugar

1 large egg

2 tablespoons finely grated lemon zest (from about 2 lemons)

3 tablespoons buttermilk

1 teaspoon fresh lemon juice

1 In a bowl, whisk together the 3 cups flour, baking soda, cream of tartar, and salt. In a large bowl, using an electric mixer on medium-high speed, beat the butter and sugar until light and fluffy, 2–3 minutes. Add the egg and lemon zest and beat on low speed until the egg is completely incorporated. Beating on low speed, slowly add the flour mixture and continue to beat until almost incorporated. Add the buttermilk and the lemon juice and beat on low speed until just incorporated, scraping down the sides of the bowl as needed.

2 Press the dough into a rough rectangle, wrap tightly in plastic wrap, and refrigerate until firm, at least 1 hour or up to overnight. (The dough can be wrapped well and frozen for up to 1 month.)

3 Follow the desired recipe for rolling and cutting, or do the following: Preheat the oven to 350°F (180°C). Line 3 baking sheets with parchment paper. On a lightly floured work surface, using a floured rolling pin, roll out the chilled dough until about ¼ inch (6 mm) thick. Using cookie cutters or a paring knife, cut the cookies into the desired shapes. Use a metal spatula to transfer the cookies to the prepared sheets, spacing them 1 inch (2.5 cm) apart. Press the dough scraps together, roll out, and cut out additional shapes.

4 Follow the desired recipe for baking and cooling, or do the following: Bake 1 sheet at a time until the cookies are lightly golden around the edges but the tops are barely colored, 12–15 minutes (or as indicated in the recipe). Let cool on the sheets for 5 minutes. Using the metal spatula, transfer to wire racks and let cool completely, about 30 minutes.

5 Decorate the cookies as desired.

To create the perfect holiday cookie, add one teaspoon each of freshly ground cinnamon and allspice and a pinch of freshly ground nutmeg to the flour mixture.

2¾ cups (14 oz/440 g) all-purpose flour, plus more for dusting

1 teaspoon baking powder

¼ teaspoon baking soda

¼ teaspoon salt

¾ cup (6 oz/185 g) plus 2 tablespoons unsalted butter, at room temperature

1 cup (7 oz/220 g) firmly packed dark brown sugar

1 large egg

1 tablespoon molasses

1 tablespoon heavy cream

BROWN SUGAR COOKIES

makes about 24 cookies

1 In a bowl, whisk together the 2¾ cups flour, baking powder, baking soda, and salt. In a large bowl, using an electric mixer on medium-high speed, beat the butter and sugar until light and fluffy, 2–3 minutes. Add the egg and molasses and beat on low speed until the egg is completely incorporated. Beating on low speed, slowly add the flour mixture and continue to beat until just incorporated, scraping down the sides of the bowl as needed. Add the cream and mix until incorporated.

2 Press the dough into a rough rectangle, wrap tightly in plastic wrap, and refrigerate until firm, at least 1 hour or up to overnight. (The dough can be wrapped well and frozen for up to 1 month.)

3 Follow the desired recipe for rolling and cutting, or do the following: Preheat the oven to 350°F (180°C). Line 3 baking sheets with parchment paper. On a lightly floured work surface, using a floured rolling pin, roll out the chilled dough until about ¼ inch (6 mm) thick. Using cookie cutters or a paring knife, cut the cookies into the desired shapes. Use a metal spatula to transfer the cookies to the prepared sheets, spacing them 1 inch (2.5 cm) apart. Press the dough scraps together, roll out, and cut out additional shapes.

4 Follow the desired recipe for baking and cooling, or do the following: Bake 1 sheet at a time until the cookies are golden brown around the edges but the tops have not yet taken on additional color, 12–15 minutes (or as indicated in the recipe). Let cool on the sheets for 5 minutes. Using the metal spatula, transfer to wire racks and let cool completely, about 30 minutes.

5 Decorate the cookies as desired.

The dark color of the dough makes it difficult to tell when the cookies are done. After the cookies have baked for 12 minutes, use a finger to test if they are firm in the center.

CHOCOLATE SUGAR COOKIES
makes about 30 cookies

1   In a bowl, whisk together the 2¼ cups flour, cocoa powder, baking powder, baking soda, and salt. In a large bowl, using an electric mixer on medium-high speed, beat the butter and sugars until light and fluffy, 2–3 minutes. Add the egg and vanilla and beat on low speed until the egg is completely incorporated. Beating on low speed, slowly add the flour mixture and continue to beat until just incorporated, scraping down the sides of the bowl as needed.

2   Press the dough into a rough rectangle, wrap tightly in plastic wrap, and refrigerate until firm, at least 1 hour or up to overnight. (The dough can be wrapped well and frozen for up to 1 month.)

3   Follow the desired recipe for rolling and cutting, or do the following: Preheat the oven to 350°F (180°C). Line 3 baking sheets with parchment paper. On a lightly floured work surface, using a floured rolling pin, roll out the chilled dough until about ¼ inch (6 mm) thick. Using cookie cutters or a paring knife, cut the cookies into the desired shapes. Use a metal spatula to transfer the cookies to the prepared sheets, spacing them 1 inch (2.5 cm) apart. Press the dough scraps together, roll out, and cut out additional shapes.

4   Follow the desired recipe for baking and cooling, or do the following: Bake 1 sheet at a time until the cookies are firm to the touch, 12–15 minutes (or as indicated in the recipe). Let cool on the sheets for 5 minutes. Using the metal spatula, transfer to wire racks and let cool completely, about 30 minutes.

5   Decorate the cookies as desired.

2¼ cups (11½ oz/360 g) all-purpose flour, plus more for dusting

⅓ cup (1 oz/30 g) unsweetened cocoa powder

½ teaspoon baking powder

½ teaspoon baking soda

¼ teaspoon salt

¾ cup (6 oz/185 g) unsalted butter, at room temperature

1 cup (7 oz/220 g) firmly packed light brown sugar

¼ cup (2 oz/60 g) granulated sugar

1 large egg

1 teaspoon pure vanilla extract

Using both fresh and ground ginger adds plenty of bold flavor to these cookies. For triple-ginger intensity, sprinkle ¼ cup (1½ oz/45 g) chopped crystallized ginger on top of iced cookies.

GINGERBREAD COOKIES
makes about 30 cookies

3 cups (15 oz/470 g) all-purpose flour, plus more for dusting

1 teaspoon baking soda

½ teaspoon baking powder

½ teaspoon salt

1½ teaspoons ground ginger

1½ teaspoons ground cinnamon

1 teaspoon ground allspice

1 cup (8 oz/250 g) unsalted butter, at room temperature

1¼ cups (9 oz/280 g) firmly packed light brown sugar

1 large egg

2 tablespoons molasses

1 tablespoon finely grated fresh ginger

1   In a bowl, whisk together the 3 cups flour, baking soda, baking powder, salt, ground ginger, cinnamon, and allspice. In a large bowl, using an electric mixer on medium-high speed, beat the butter and brown sugar until light and fluffy, 2–3 minutes. Add the egg, molasses, and fresh ginger and beat on low speed until the egg is completely incorporated. Beating on low speed, slowly add the flour mixture and continue to beat until just incorporated, scraping down the sides of the bowl as needed.

2   Press the dough into a rough rectangle, wrap tightly in plastic wrap, and refrigerate until firm, at least 1 hour or up to overnight. (The dough can be wrapped well and frozen for up to 1 month.)

3   Follow the desired recipe for rolling and cutting, or do the following: Preheat the oven to 350°F (180°C). Line 3 baking sheets with parchment paper. On a lightly floured work surface, using a floured rolling pin, roll out the chilled dough until about ¼ inch (6 mm) thick. Using cookie cutters or as directed in the recipe, cut the cookies into the desired shapes. Use a metal spatula to transfer the cookies to the prepared sheets, spacing them 1 inch (2.5 cm) apart. Press the dough scraps together, roll out, and cut out additional shapes.

4   Follow the desired recipe for baking and cooling, or do the following: Bake 1 sheet at a time until the cookies begin to turn a shade darker around the edges and are firm to the touch, 12–15 minutes (or as indicated in the recipe). Let cool on the sheets for 5 minutes. Using the metal spatula, transfer to wire racks and let cool completely, about 30 minutes.

5   Decorate the cookies as desired.

Pretty flower-shaped cookies in assorted colors and forms will be the hit at any cookie exchange; here is an opportunity to get creative with whatever colors, shapes, and designs you like.

GARDEN FLOWERS

makes 30—40 cookies

1   Bake the cookies according to the Vanilla Sugar Cookies recipe, grouping like-sized cookies together; 12–15 minutes for smaller cookies and 16–19 minutes for larger ones. Let cool, about 30 minutes.

2   Depending on how many color combinations you want, divide the icing among small bowls. Add a very small amount of food coloring to each bowl and mix well (if needed, add more food coloring until the desired color is reached). Spoon each batch of icing into separate paper cones or pastry bags with ⅛-inch (3-mm) round tips (page 15). Pipe the icing around the edge of each cookie to form a border.

3   Using the same color or a contrasting color, pipe the icing into the middle of the cookie, letting it run to the edges of the border. Gently tap the cookie twice to settle the icing. If desired, sprinkle all over with sanding sugar.

4   To create a two-tone appearance, wait for the initial layer of icing to harden, about 2 hours. Cover and refrigerate the icing until needed; stir vigorously before use. Pipe an outline or accent of contrasting color on top of the first layer of icing or the sanding sugar.

5   After the accent layer of icing has almost dried, about 1 hour, choose another contrasting color and pipe a circle in the middle of each cookie. If desired, use another contrasting color to pipe small dots on top of the circle. (Alternatively, sanding sugar can also be sprinkled in the center.) Let the cookies dry completely, at least 6 hours or up to overnight.

6   Store the cookies in an airtight container, layered between sheets of parchment paper, at room temperature for up to 3 days.

Dough for Vanilla Sugar Cookies (page 18), cut into 30 large or 40 small flower shapes

Royal Icing (page 116)

Gel-paste food coloring in desired colors (page 11)

Sanding sugars for sprinkling

TOOLS NEEDED

Assorted flower-shaped cookie cutters; 4—6 paper cones or pastry bags with ⅛-inch (3-mm) round tips

There is no hiding what's inside these sandwich cookies—the filling is showcased through a center window. Jam or preserves can be used in place of the lemon curd.

LEMON WINDOW PANES
makes about 28 cookies

Dough for Vanilla Sugar Cookies (page 18), cut into 1½-by-2¼-inch (4-by-5.5-cm) rectangles

Confectioner's sugar for dusting

Lemon Curd (page 120)

TOOLS NEEDED
1½-by-2¼-inch (4-by-5.5-cm) rectangular cookie cutter; paring knife

1   Line 3 baking sheets with parchment paper.

2   With the dough rectangles still on the work surface, and working with half of the rectangles, use a small cookie cutter in a desired shape (such as a diamond) or a sharp paring knife to cut out a smaller shape in the center of half of the rectangles to create a window. Use a metal spatula to transfer the cookies to the prepared sheets, spacing them 1 inch (2.5 cm) apart. Chill in the refrigerator or freezer until firm, about 15 minutes.

3   Bake the cookies according to the Vanilla Sugar Cookies recipe for 12–15 minutes. Let cool completely, about 30 minutes.

4   Turn the solid cookies bottom side up. Spoon a rounded teaspoonful of curd in the center and swirl to spread slightly. If serving right away, dust the cutout cookies with confectioner's sugar. Gently press the dusted cookies, sugared side up, on the curd filling.

5   Store the cookies in a singer layer, in an airtight container, in the refrigerator for up to 3 days. Dust with confectioner's sugar just before serving.

Swirls of jam in the center of these cookies keep them soft and chewy on the inside, while the exterior remains crisp. You can vary the filling by using your favorite jam.

JAM SWIRLS
makes about 30 cookies

All-purpose flour for dusting

Dough for Vanilla Sugar Cookies (page 18)

2 cups (20 oz/625 g) strawberry jam

¼ cup (2 oz/60 g) sanding sugar or granulated sugar

TOOLS NEEDED
Offset spatula; chef's knife

1   Preheat the oven to 350°F (180°C). Line 3 baking sheets with parchment paper.

2   On a lightly floured work surface, using a floured rolling pin, roll the dough into a 16-by-12-inch (40-by-30-cm) rectangle about ¼ inch (6 mm) thick. Starting at the short end closest to you and using an offset spatula, evenly spread 1 cup (10 oz/310 g) of the jam over half of the dough, leaving a ½-inch (12-mm) border. Starting at the end covered in jam, roll up the dough tightly until you reach the center point of the dough forming a log.

3   Carefully invert the dough, flipping the log so that the long portion of dough not covered in jam is on your right and the rolled log is now on your left. Evenly spread the remaining 1 cup of jam onto the other half of the dough. Roll up the dough, tightly forming a log, until you reach the center of the dough. The two rolls should be rolled up in opposite directions, meeting in the center. Gently press the two rolls together. Use a chef's knife to trim the uneven ends. Refrigerate or freeze the log until firm, about 10 minutes.

4   Using a sharp knife, cut the roll crosswise into 30 slices about ½ inch thick. Use a metal spatula to transfer the slices to the prepared sheets, spacing them 1½ inches (4 cm) apart. Sprinkle each cookie with sugar.

5   Bake the cookies until lightly golden around the edges and the tops are barely colored, 16–19 minutes. Let cool completely, about 30 minutes.

6   Store the cookies in an airtight container, layered between sheets of parchment paper, at room temperature for up to 4 days.

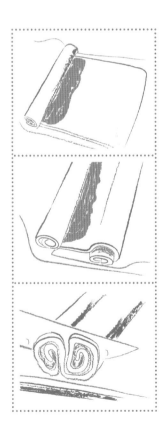

If you prefer both chocolate and vanilla flavors in one cookie, keep the cookies whole, then dip half of each cookie in the icing and let it set up before dipping the other half in chocolate.

Dough for Vanilla Sugar Cookies (page 18), cut into 2¾-inch (6.5-cm) rounds

Royal Icing (page 116)

Chocolate Glaze (page 116)

TOOLS NEEDED

2¾-inch (6.5-cm) round cookie cutter; chef's knife

BLACK & WHITE SLICES
makes about 50 cookies

1   Preheat the oven to 350°F (180°C). Line 3 baking sheets with parchment paper.

2   Arrange the dough rounds on a work surface. Using a chef's knife, cut each round in half. Use a metal spatula to transfer the cookies to the prepared sheets, spacing them 1 inch (2.5 cm) apart.

3   Bake the cookies according to the Vanilla Sugar Cookies recipe for 12–15 minutes. Let cool completely, about 30 minutes. Reserve the parchment-lined baking sheets.

4   If needed, adjust the consistency of the icing by stirring in a small amount of warm water so that it coats the back of a spoon but still runs off the edges smoothly. Using 2 forks to carefully hold a cookie, dip it into the icing and gently tap it to remove any excess. Place on one of the reserved parchment-lined baking sheets. Repeat to coat half of the cookies with the icing.

5   If needed, adjust the consistency of the glaze by placing it in a heatproof bowl set over (but not touching) simmering water until it has thinned slightly, about 1 minute. Remove from the heat and stir. Repeat the coating process by using 2 forks to carefully hold a cookie, dip it into the glaze and gently tap to remove any excess. Place on the second parchment-lined sheet. Repeat to coat the remaining cookies with the glaze.

6   Refrigerate the coated cookies on the sheet pans until set, at least 20 minutes. Store in an airtight container, layered between sheets of parchment paper, in the refrigerator for up to 3 days.

The inspiration for the design on these cookies came from the beautiful details found on ceramic tiles. You can duplicate the patterns here or create your own using contrasting colors.

CERAMIC TILE COOKIES

makes about 20 cookies

Dough for Vanilla Sugar Cookies (page 18), cut into 3-inch (7.5-cm) squares

Royal Icing (page 116)

Gel-paste food coloring in 2 desired colors (page 11)

TOOLS NEEDED

3-inch (7.5-cm) square cookie cutter; 3 paper cones or pastry bags with ¼-inch (6-mm) round tips; toothpicks

1 Bake the cookies according to the Vanilla Sugar Cookies recipe for 16–19 minutes. Let cool completely, about 30 minutes.

2 Spoon ¼ cup (2 fl oz/60 ml) of the icing into a small bowl and another ¼ cup into another small bowl. Add a very small amount of food coloring to each bowl and mix well (if needed, add more food coloring until the desired color is reached). Spoon into separate paper cones or pastry bags, each with a ⅛-inch (3-mm) round tip (page 15).

3 Spoon the remaining white icing into a paper cone or pastry bag with a ¼-inch (6-mm) plain round tip (page 15). Pipe the white icing around the edge of each cookie to form a border. Then, pipe more white icing into the middle of the cookie, letting it run to the edges of the border (see illustrations on page 25). Gently tap the cookie twice to settle the icing. Let the cookies firm up for at least 2 hours. Cover and refrigerate the icing until needed; stir vigorously before use.

4 Pipe straight-line borders, dots, and squares in the center of the cookies, filling some squares in with a contrasting color. To make petal shapes, pipe a large dot and, without putting any pressure on the paper cone or pastry bag, slowly pull the tip toward the edge of the cookie, dragging some of the icing. You can also use the tip of a toothpick to gently drag a dot of icing outward to create a petal. Let the cookies dry completely, at least 6 hours or up to overnight.

5 Store the cookies in an airtight container, layered between sheets of parchment paper, at room temperature for up to 3 days.

Packaged in cellophane with a ribbon, these petits fours would make an elegant wedding favor. Instead of sending guests home with a slice of cake, give them their own delicious cookies.

Dough for Vanilla Sugar Cookies (page 18), cut into 25 large rounds, 25 medium rounds, and 25 small rounds

Royal Icing (page 116)

Yellow, red, and pink gel-paste food coloring (page 11)

Assorted sanding sugars for decorating (optional)

25 marzipan or candy roses (optional; page 123 or purchased)

TOOLS NEEDED

2-inch (5-cm); 1½-inch (4-cm); and 1-inch (2.5-cm) round cookie cutters; 3 paper cones or pastry bags with ¼-inch (6-mm) plain round tips; toothpicks

PETITS FOURS
makes about 25 cookies

1   Preheat the oven to 350°F (180°C). Line 3 baking sheets with parchment paper. Using a metal spatula, transfer the dough rounds to the baking sheets, grouping like-sized cookies together. Bake until the cookies are golden around the edges, 8–10 minutes for smaller cookies, 16–19 minutes for larger ones. Let cool completely, about 30 minutes.

2   Spoon ¾ cup (6 fl oz/180 ml) of the icing into a small bowl. Add a very small amount of yellow food coloring and mix well (if needed, add more food coloring until the desired color is reached). Spoon ¾ cup each of the remaining icing into two small bowls and follow the same steps to make light pink and dark pink colors. Spoon each of the colored icings into paper cones or pastry bags with ¼-inch (6-mm) round tips (page 15).

3   Pipe the yellow icing around the edge of the 2-inch cookies to form a border. Then pipe the icing into the middle of the cookie, letting it run to the edges of the border (see illustrations on page 25). Gently tap each cookie twice to settle the icing. Repeat the process to ice the 1½-inch cookies with the light pink icing and the 1-inch cookies with the dark pink icing. Let the cookies dry completely, at least 6 hours or up to overnight. Cover and refrigerate the icing until needed again; stir vigorously before use. Sprinkle each cookie with sanding sugar, if using.

4   Pipe a ½-inch (12-mm) dot of icing in the center of each 2-inch cookie and top with a 1½-inch cookie. Pipe another ½-inch dot of icing in the center and top with a 1-inch cookie. Pipe a small dot of icing in the center and top with a marzipan rose, if using. Pipe pink dots on each tier. Let the assembled cookies dry completely, at least 2 hours.

5   These cookies should be stored in a single layer, in an airtight container at room temperature for up to 3 days.

If you can't find the ideal cookie cutter, trace or print letters on card stock and cut them out with a utility knife or scissors. Place them on the dough and cut shapes with the tip of a paring knife.

ALPHABET COOKIES
makes about 24 cookies

1   Bake the cookies according to the Vanilla Sugar Cookies recipe, for 16–19 minutes. Let cool completely, about 30 minutes.

2   Spoon the icing into a bowl and add food coloring, if using. Spoon into a paper cone or pastry bag with a ⅛-inch (3-mm) round tip (page 15). Pipe the icing around the edge of each cookie to form a border. Then pipe the icing into the middle of the cookie, letting it run to the edges of the border (see illustrations on page 25). Gently tap the cookie twice to settle the icing. Top each cookie with sanding sugar or sprinkles, if desired.

3   Set the cookies aside to firm up for at least 2 hours or up to overnight.

4   Store the cookies in an airtight container, layered between sheets of parchment paper, at room temperature for up to 3 days.

Dough for Vanilla Sugar Cookies (page 18), cut into alphabet shapes

Royal Icing (page 116)

Food coloring (optional)

Assorted sanding sugars or sprinkles for decorating

TOOLS NEEDED

Alphabet cookie cutters; 1 paper cone or pastry bag with a ⅛-inch (3-mm) round tip

This recipe uses half of the chocolate dough. The remaining half can be frozen for up to 1 month. Slice the dough directly from the freezer and then bake the cookies.

Dough for Vanilla Sugar Cookies (page 18)

Pink food coloring

Orange food coloring

Dough for Chocolate Sugar Cookies (page 21)

White sanding sugar

TOOLS NEEDED

Chef's knife

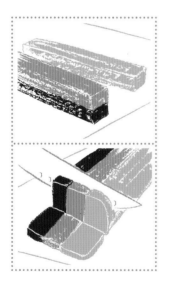

NEAPOLITANS
makes about 40 cookies

1 Divide the vanilla dough in half. Add 1 to 2 drops pink food coloring to one half and 1–2 drops orange food coloring to the other half. Knead each piece of dough separately until the color is completely incorporated. Divide the chocolate dough in half. Wrap each dough in plastic wrap and refrigerate until well chilled, about 30 minutes.

2 Once chilled, shape one half of the chocolate dough into a rectangular log 12 inches (30 cm) long, 1½ inches (4 cm) wide, and ¾ inch (2 cm) thick. (Reserve the other half in the refrigerator or freezer for another use.) Shape the pink dough and orange dough into logs of the same size. Stack the logs on top of each other, placing the pink in the middle. Gently press the logs together to seal. Wrap tightly in plastic wrap and refrigerate until firm, about 1 hour.

3 Preheat the oven to 350°F (180°C). Line 3 baking sheets with parchment paper.

4 Using a chef's knife, trim the edges of the log to create a perfect rectangular shape. Brush the dough with water and roll in sanding sugar to coat. Cut the dough crosswise into slices ¼ inch (6 mm) thick. Using a metal spatula, transfer the slices to the prepared sheets, spacing them 1 inch (2.5 cm) apart.

5 Bake 1 batch at a time until the center of each cookie feels firm to the touch but has not yet taken on any golden color, 12–15 minutes. Let cool on the sheets for 5 minutes. Using the metal spatula, transfer to wire racks and let cool completely, about 30 minutes.

6 Store the cookies, layered between sheets of parchment paper, in an airtight container at room temperature for up to 3 days.

Pressing soft dough through a ricer creates the distinctive texture of these cookies. Make the dough just before you shape the cookies. If using frozen dough, let it sit out at room temperature for 1 hour.

BIRD'S NESTS
makes about 15 cookies

1 Use the tip of a toothpick to add a very small amount of food coloring to the marzipan. Knead until the color is evenly distributed. (It will turn slightly green because the marzipan is beige, not white.) To make each egg, roll a teaspoonful of the marzipan into a ball, then roll the ends slightly to create an oval. (The eggs can be prepared 1 week in advance and stored in an airtight container at room temperature.)

2 Line 3 baking sheets with parchment paper.

3 Place a tennis ball-sized mound of dough in a handheld ricer and firmly squeeze, extruding the dough over the prepared sheets. Use a metal spatula to scrape the dough strands from the ricer. Using 2 forks, carefully form round nests about 3 inches (7.5 cm) in diameter from the riced dough. With the back of a spoon, firmly press an indentation in the center of each nest. Repeat with the remaining dough. Sprinkle the nests with sanding sugar. Chill in the refrigerator or freezer until firm, about 15 minutes.

4 Bake the cookies according to the Brown Sugar Cookies recipe, for 12–15 minutes. Let cool completely, about 40 minutes.

5 Use a vegetable peeler to shave curls from the chocolate. Arrange a few curls in the nests and top with the marzipan eggs.

6 Store the cookies, in a single layer, in an airtight container at room temperature for up to 3 days.

Dough for Brown Sugar Cookies (page 20)

5 oz (155 g) marzipan or small chocolate eggs

Blue gel-paste food coloring (page 11)

White sanding sugar for sprinkling

Block of bittersweet chocolate for shaving

TOOLS NEEDED

Handheld ricer; toothpick; vegetable peeler

These cookies are shaped like irregular marble slabs, with the green decoration imitating the veining in the stone. You can also bake the cookies in oval shapes and turn them into marbleized eggs.

All-purpose flour for dusting

Dough for Vanilla Sugar Cookies (page 18)

Royal Icing (page 116)

Green gel-paste food coloring (page 11)

TOOLS NEEDED

Pizza wheel; 3 paper cones or pastry bags with ¼-inch (6-mm) round tips; toothpicks

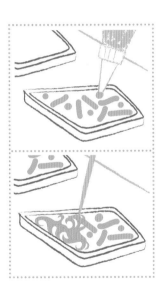

MARBLE SLABS
makes about 24 cookies

1 Line 3 baking sheets with parchment paper.

2 On a lightly floured work surface, using a floured rolling pin, roll the dough to about ¼ inch (6 mm) thick. Using a pizza wheel, cut pieces of various sizes. Use a metal spatula to transfer the cookies to the prepared sheets, grouping like-sized cookies together and spacing them 1 inch (2.5 cm) apart. Press the dough scraps together, roll out, and cut more shapes. Chill in the refrigerator until firm, about 15 minutes.

3 Bake the cookies according to the Vanilla Sugar Cookies recipe, for 16–19 minutes. Let cool completely, about 30 minutes.

4 Spoon ¼ cup (2 fl oz/60 ml) of the icing into a small bowl and another ¼ cup into another small bowl. Add a very small amount of food coloring to color each a shade of green, one lighter than the other. Spoon into separate paper cones or pastry bags, each with a ¼-inch round tip. Spoon the remaining white icing into a pastry bag fitted with a ¼-inch plain round tip (page 15).

5 Pipe the white icing around the edge of each cookie to form a border. Then pipe the icing into the middle of the cookie, letting it run to the edges of the border. While the icing is still wet, pipe various sizes of dots and lines in the 2 shades of green on top of the white icing. Using a toothpick or wooden skewer, quickly swirl the colors together, making only 8 to 10 figure-eight motions and stopping before the colors are completely combined. Gently tap each cookie once or twice to settle the icing. Let the cookies dry completely, at least 6 hours or up to overnight.

6 Store the cookies in an airtight container, layered between sheets of parchment paper, at room temperature for up to 3 days.

These cookies look luminous when hung where the light can sparkle through them. Avoid making them on a humid or rainy day to ensure that the sugar centers harden properly.

STAINED GLASS COOKIES

makes about 30 cookies

1   Line 3 baking sheets with parchment paper.

2   Using smaller cookie cutters, cut a window from each shape. Use a metal spatula to transfer the cookies to the prepared sheets, spacing them 1 inch (2.5 cm) apart. Press the dough scraps together, roll out, and cut out additional shapes. Use a skewer or drinking straw to cut a small hole in the top of each cookie if you intend to hang it. Chill the cookies in the refrigerator or freezer until firm, about 15 minutes.

3   Bake the cookies according to the Vanilla Sugar Cookies recipe for 16–19 minutes. Let cool completely, about 30 minutes. While the cookies are cooling on the wire racks, spray the parchment-lined sheets with nonstick cooking spray, then place the cooled cookies on the sheets.

4   In a saucepan over medium-high heat, bring the sugar, the corn syrup, and ½ cup (4 fl oz/125 ml) water to a boil and continue to cook until the sugar mixture registers 300°F (150°C) on a candy thermometer. Remove from the heat and divide into separate heatproof measuring cups (if making more than one color). Using a wooden spoon, carefully stir in 1 drop food coloring and the extract, if using. Slowly pour the sugar mixture into the cutout center of each cookie, filling it to the thickness of the cookie. Let cool until the center of each cookie has hardened, about 30 minutes.

5   If hanging the cookies, thread a ribbon through the hole in each cookie. Store the cookies in an airtight container at room temperature for up to 2 days.

Dough for Vanilla Sugar Cookies (page 18), cut into various shapes

2 cups (1 lb/500 g) sugar

¼ cup (2½ fl oz/75 ml) light corn syrup

Nonstick cooking spray

Gel-paste food coloring in desired colors (page 11)

½ teaspoon flavoring extract such as vanilla or almond (optional)

TOOLS NEEDED

Assorted nesting sets of cookie cutters; skewer; candy thermometer; ribbon

Here, an abstract pattern of arcs is piped onto royal icing creating a canvas, which also gives these cookies a sophisticated elegance. You can use the colors shown here or create your own combinations.

Dough for Vanilla Sugar Cookies (page 18), cut into 3-inch (7.5-cm) squares

Royal Icing (page 116)

Purple, yellow, and green gel-paste food coloring (page 11)

TOOLS NEEDED

Paring knife; 3-inch (7.5-cm) square cookie cutter; 2 paper cones or pastry bags with ⅛-inch (3-mm) round tips; 1 paper cone or pastry bag with ¼-inch (6-mm) round tip

ABSTRACT ART COOKIES
makes about 30 cookies

1   Line 3 baking sheets with parchment paper.

2   Use a sharp paring knife to cut half of the squares in half to make rectangles. Use a metal spatula to transfer the cookies to the prepared sheets, grouping like-sized cookies together and spacing them 1 inch (2.5 cm) apart. Chill in the refrigerator or freezer until firm, about 15 minutes.

3   Bake the cookies according to the Vanilla Sugar Cookies recipe for 16–19 minutes. Let cool completely, about 30 minutes.

4   Spoon ¼ cup (2 fl oz/60 ml) of the icing into a small bowl and another ¼ cup into another bowl. Add a small amount of food coloring to color one a deep shade of purple. Color the other chartreuse by adding 1 or 2 drops yellow food coloring and, using a toothpick to mix in the color, a tiny dot of green. Spoon into separate paper cones or pastry bags, each with a ⅛-inch (3-mm) round tip. Spoon the remaining white icing into a paper cone or pastry bag with a ¼-inch (6-mm) round tip (page 15).

5   Pipe the white icing around the edge of each cookie to form a border. Then pipe the icing into the middle of the cookie, letting it run to the edges of the border (see illustrations on page 25). Gently tap the cookie twice to settle the icing. Set aside to firm up, at least 2 hours.

6   Pipe arcs of purple and chartreuse icing on the cookies, stopping at the edge of one cookie and then picking up the pattern at the edge of the next cookie. Let the cookies dry, at least 6 hours or up to overnight.

7   Store the cookies in an airtight container, layered between sheets of parchment paper, at room temperature for up to 3 days.

These cookies serve a dual purpose: as a sophisticated way to seat guests and as a delicious edible favor. They can be made in advance and placed in a cellophane bag secured with a ribbon.

PLACE CARD COOKIES

makes about 24 cookies

1   Preheat the oven to 350°F (180°C). Line 3 baking sheets with parchment paper.

2   On a lightly floured work surface, using a floured rolling pin, roll the dough into a 15-by-12-inch (38-by-30-cm) rectangle about ¼ inch (6 mm) thick. Using a ruler as a straightedge and a pizza wheel, cut twenty-four 3½-by-2-inch (9-by-5-cm) rectangles. Use a metal spatula to transfer the cookies to the prepared sheets, spacing them 1 inch (2.5 cm) apart. Chill in the refrigerator or freezer until firm, about 15 minutes.

3   Bake the cookies according to the Vanilla Sugar Cookies recipe for 16–19 minutes. Let cool completely, about 30 minutes.

4   Place ¼ cup (2 fl oz/60 ml) each of the icing into two small bowls. Add a very small amount of food coloring to color each a shade of blue, one lighter than the other. Spoon each of the blue icings into a paper cone or pastry bag with a ⅛-inch (3-mm) round tip. Spoon the remaining white icing into a paper cone or a pastry bag with a ¼-inch (6-mm) round tip (page 15). Using the white icing, pipe around the edge of each cookie to form a border, then pipe into the middle of the cookie, letting it run to the edges of the border (see illustrations on page 25). Gently tap the cookie twice to settle the icing. Set aside to firm up, at least 2 hours. Using one of the blue icings, pipe straight-line borders around the cookie, accenting with the dots. In the center of each cookie, pipe a name, in both blue colors, first the dark, then the light. Let the cookies dry at least 6 hours or overnight. Cover and refrigerate the icing until needed; stir vigorously before use.

5   Store the cookies in an airtight container, layered between sheets of parchment paper, at room temperature for up to 3 days.

All-purpose flour for dusting

Dough for Vanilla Sugar Cookies (page 18)

Royal Icing (page 116)

Gel-paste food coloring, blue and turquoise (page 11)

TOOLS NEEDED

Ruler, pizza wheel; 2 paper cones or piping bags with ⅛-inch (3-mm) round tips; 1 paper cone or pastry bag with a ¼-inch (6-mm) round tip

The blocks of color on these cookies are defined by the zigzag imprint of a fluted pastry wheel. You can duplicate the colors used here or come up with your own creative combination.

ZIGZAG SQUARES

makes about 20 cookies

Dough for Vanilla Sugar Cookies (page 18), cut into 3-inch (7.5-cm) squares

Royal Icing (page 116)

Pink and green gel-paste food coloring (page 11)

TOOLS NEEDED

3-inch (7.5-cm) square cookie cutter; fluted pastry wheel; 3 paper cones or pastry bags with ¼-inch (6-mm) round tips

1   Line 3 baking sheets with parchment paper.

2   Using a fluted pastry wheel, press an irregular grid into each cookie, being careful not to press all the way through the dough. Using a metal spatula, transfer the cookies to the prepared baking sheet. Chill in the refrigerator or freezer until firm, about 15 minutes.

3   Bake the cookies according to the recipe for Vanilla Sugar Cookies for 16–19 minutes. Let cool completely, about 30 minutes.

4   Spoon one-third of the icing into a paper cone or pastry bag with a ¼-inch (6-mm) round tip. Spoon half of the remaining icing into a small bowl and the other half into another small bowl. Using a very small amount of food coloring, tint one a pale shade of pink and the other pale green. Spoon into separate paper cones or pastry bags, each with a ¼-inch round tip (page 15). Using the white icing, outline 1 or 2 compartments of each cookie bordered by the fluted imprint. Then pipe icing into the middle of the cookie, letting it run to the edges of the border (see illustrations on page 25). Repeat to fill the remaining compartments, using the pink and green icings. Gently tap the cookie twice to settle the icing. Let the cookies dry at least 6 hours or up to overnight.

5   Store the cookies in an airtight container, layered between sheets of parchment paper, at room temperature for up to 3 days.

Once the initial rounds of dough are cut, the centers are removed with progressively smaller cookie cutters, and the contrasting colors are swapped to create the appearance of concentric rings.

TREE RINGS
makes about 24 cookies

1   Line 3 baking sheets with parchment paper.

2   On a lightly floured work surface, using a floured rolling pin, roll out the gingerbread dough until about ½ inch (12 mm) thick. Using a 2¾-inch (7-cm) round cookie cutter, cut out as many shapes as possible. Using a metal spatula, transfer the cookies to the prepared sheets, spacing them 1 inch (2.5 cm) apart. Press the dough scraps together, roll out, and cut out additional shapes. Repeat with the vanilla dough.

3   Use a 2½-inch (6-cm) round cookie cutter to cut the center from each 2¾-inch round. Next, place the centers of the gingerbread rounds into the centers of the vanilla rounds and the centers of the vanilla rounds into the centers of the gingerbread rounds. Continue to cut the centers from the cookies, using progressively smaller cutters and swapping them. The smallest hole can be made using a drinking straw. Gently press the cookies with the palm of your hand to help the dough rings adhere to each other. Chill in the refrigerator or freezer until firm, about 15 minutes.

4   Preheat the oven to 350°F (180°C). Bake 1 sheet at a time until the cookies are lightly golden around the edges, 20–22 minutes. Let cool on the sheets for 5 minutes. Using the metal spatula, transfer to wire racks and let cool completely, about 30 minutes.

5   Brush some glaze around each cookie. Wrap a strip of the marzipan, if using, around the cookie, trimming any excess. Refrigerate the cookies for at least 20 minutes before serving. Store in an airtight container, between sheets of parchment paper, in the refrigerator for up to 2 days.

All-purpose flour for dusting

Dough for Gingerbread Cookies (page 22)

Dough for Vanilla Sugar Cookies (page 18)

Confectioner's sugar for dusting

Chocolate Glaze (page 116)

Marzipan Bark (optional; page 122)

TOOLS NEEDED

Nesting set of round cookie cutters; drinking straw

Polka dots never go out of style. In addition to decorating with different shades of yellow, you can use round cutters of varying diameters. Stir lemon extract into the icing for more lemon flavor.

Dough for Lemon-Buttermilk Cookies (page 19), cut into various sized rounds

Royal Icing (page 116)

Gel-paste food coloring in various shades of yellow (page 11)

TOOLS NEEDED

Assorted round cookie cutters, toothpicks; 3 or 4 paper cones or pastry bags with ¼-inch (6-mm) round tips

POLKA DOTS
makes about 32 cookies

1 Bake the cookies according to the Lemon-Buttermilk Cookies recipe for 12–15 minutes, grouping like-sized cookies together. Let cool completely, about 30 minutes.

2 Spoon one-fourth of the icing into a paper cone or pastry bag with a ¼-inch (6-mm) round tip. Divide the remaining icing into thirds and place in separate small bowls. Use the tip of a toothpick to add food coloring to each bowl, making each a different shade of yellow. Spoon into separate paper cones or pastry bags, each with ¼-inch round tips (page 15). Pipe the white icing around the edge of each cookie to form a border. Then pipe the icing into the middle of the cookie letting it run to the edges of the border. While the icing is still wet, pipe dots of various sizes in each shade of yellow into the white icing. Gently tap the cookie to settle the icing. Let the cookies dry completely, at least 6 hours or up to overnight.

3 Store the cookies in an airtight container, layered between sheets of parchment paper, at room temperature for up to 3 days.

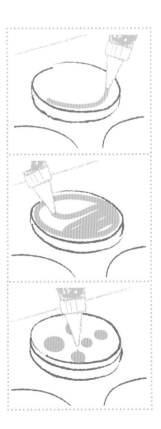

Made in miniature tartlet tins, these cookies bake crisp on the outside from the sanding sugar, but stay soft and moist inside like cake. Serve the little cakes topped with a dollop of whipped cream.

TARTLET TIN COOKIES
makes about 28 cookies

1 Preheat the oven to 350°F (180°C).

2 Place miniature tartlet tins, each about 1½ inches (4 cm) in diameter, on 2 rimmed baking sheets. Lightly brush each tin with the butter. Sprinkle generously with sanding sugar. Firmly press 1 rounded tablespoon of dough into each prepared tin, filling it three-fourths full.

3 Bake 1 batch at a time until the edges are set and the cookies feel firm to the touch, but have not yet taken on any golden color, 16–18 minutes. Let cool on the sheets on wire racks for 5 minutes. Using tongs if the tart tins are still warm, invert the tins and gently tap to remove the cookies. Use a metal spatula to transfer the cookies to the wire racks and let cool completely, about 30 minutes.

4 Dust the cooled cookies with confectioner's sugar and serve right away; the cookies are best eaten the same day they are made.

Dough for Vanilla Sugar Cookies (page 18)

¼ cup (2 oz/60 g) unsalted butter, softened

Pink and yellow sanding sugar

Confectioner's sugar for dusting

Whipped cream (optional)

TOOLS NEEDED
Tartlet tins in various shapes

Make the dough just before you are ready to roll and shape it, as cold dough will tend to crack when folding. If using chilled dough, let it sit out at room temperature for 1 hour to soften before use.

1 large egg white

All-purpose flour for dusting

Dough for Vanilla Sugar Cookies (page 18)

White sanding sugar for sprinkling

1¼ cups (15 oz/420 g) blackberry jam or preserves

TOOLS NEEDED
Ruler; pizza wheel

PINWHEELS
makes 24 cookies

1 Preheat the oven to 350°F (180°C). Line 3 baking sheets with parchment paper. In a small bowl, whisk together the egg white and 2 teaspoons water, and set aside.

2 On a lightly floured work surface, using a floured rolling pin, roll the dough into an 11-by-16-inch (28-by-40-cm) rectangle about ¼ inch (6 mm) thick. Using a ruler as a straightedge and a pizza wheel or paring knife, trim the edges of the dough to form a 10-by-15-inch (25-by-38-cm) rectangle. Then cut the dough into twenty-four 2½-inch (6-cm) squares.

3 Use a metal spatula to transfer the cookies to the prepared sheets, spacing them 1 inch (2.5 cm) apart. Using the pizza wheel or a sharp paring knife, make diagonal cuts from each corner three-fourths of the way toward the center of each square. Each corner should have 2 points. Fold every other point toward the center, gently pressing it down to seal. Lightly brush the cookies with the egg white mixture. Sprinkle with sanding sugar. Spoon 1 tablespoon of the jam into the center of each cookie.

4 Bake until the cookies are lightly golden brown around the edges and just barely golden near the center, 16–19 minutes. Let cool on the sheets for 5 minutes. Using the metal spatula, transfer to wire racks and let cool completely, about 30 minutes.

5 Store the cookies, layered between sheets or parchment paper, in an airtight container at room temperature for up to 3 days.

The colorful swirling pattern on these cookies looks complicated but is quite easy to do. Mix and match the colors to your liking and be sure to let the cookies dry completely before packing them up.

FIRE & ICE COOKIES

makes about 28 cookies

1   Bake the cookies according to the Vanilla Sugar Cookies recipe for 16–19 minutes. Let cool completely, about 30 minutes.

2   Place ¼ cup (2 fl oz/60 ml) of the icing into each of 3 small bowls. Add a very small amount of food coloring to each bowl, making one red, another orange, and the third yellow. Spoon into separate paper cones or pastry bags, each with a ¼-inch (6-mm) round tip. Spoon the remaining white icing into a paper cone or pastry bag with a ¼-inch round tip (page 15). Pipe the white icing around the edge of each cookie to form a border. Then pipe the icing into the middle of the cookie, letting it run to the edges of the border. Gently tap the cookie twice to settle the icing.

3   While the icing is still wet, pipe two 2½-inch (6-cm) lines of red icing about 1 inch (2.5 cm) from the top of each cookie. Directly below these, pipe two 2½-inch lines of orange icing. Repeat with the yellow icing and finish with 2 more lines of red icing. Drag a toothpick from the top red lines through to the bottom red lines. Wipe the toothpick clean, and then drag it from the bottom to the top, about ½ inch (12 mm) from the first swirl. Continue dragging the toothpick through the lines of icing, moving in opposite directions and wiping the toothpick clean each time. Let the cookies dry for at least 6 hours or up to overnight.

4   Store the cookies in an airtight container, layered between sheets of parchment paper, at room temperature for up to 3 days.

Dough for Vanilla Sugar Cookies (page 18), cut into 3-inch (7.5-cm) rounds

Royal Icing (page 116)

Red, orange, and yellow gel-paste food coloring (page 11)

TOOLS NEEDED

3-inch (7.5-cm) round cookie cutter; toothpicks; 4 paper cones or pastry bags with ¼-inch (6-mm) round tips

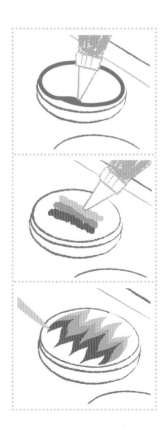

For use as a guide when cutting the dough, prepare a template by tracing a paisley shape on parchment paper. Place the template on the rolled dough and cut around it with the tip of a paring knife.

All-purpose flour for dusting

Dough for Gingerbread Cookies (page 22), cut into paisley shapes (see note)

Royal Icing (page 116)

Red and brown gel-paste food coloring

Dragées (see page 11)

½ teaspoon silver luster dust

Orange extract

TOOLS NEEDED

Toothpicks; 2 paper cones or pastry bags with ¼-inch (6-mm) round tips; tweezers, paint brush

PAISLEY COOKIES
makes about 32 cookies

1　Bake the cookies according to the Gingerbread Cookies recipe 12–15 minutes. Let cool completely, about 30 minutes.

2　Spoon one-third of the icing into a small bowl and add 2–3 drops of red food coloring. Using the tip of a toothpick, add a small amount of brown food coloring to make a maroon color. Spoon the maroon icing into a paper cone or pastry bag with a ¼-inch (6-mm) round tip (page 15). Spoon the remaining icing into a bowl and use the tip of a toothpick to add a small amount of red food coloring, coloring it pink. Spoon the pink icing into a paper cone or pastry bag with a ¼-inch round tip.

3　Pipe the maroon icing around the edge of each cookie to form a thick border. Then pipe the pink icing into the middle of the cookie, letting it run to the edges of the border (see illustrations on page 25). Gently tap the cookie twice to settle the icing. Set the cookies aside to firm up for at least 2 hours or up to overnight. Cover and refrigerate the icing until needed; stir vigorously before use. Pipe dots of maroon icing on the maroon border and a large maroon dot at the widest end of the paisley shape. Use tweezers to set 3 dragées in the large dot. Let the cookies dry completely, at least 4 hours or up to overnight.

4　In a small bowl, combine the silver luster dust and 1 drop orange extract. Stir with a clean paintbrush until the mixture is the consistency of sour cream. Brush the silver luster onto each maroon dot around the dragées. Let dry for about 1 hour.

5　Store the cookies in an airtight container, layered between sheets of parchment paper, at room temperature for up to 3 days.

The best sandwich cookies are soft enough to bite through without the filling squeezing out. To achieve this, slightly underbake the cookies. The cookies will also soften after they are refrigerated.

CHOCOLATE SWEETHEARTS

makes about 30 cookies

1   Sprinkle the cookies with the sanding sugar, if using, and bake according to the Chocolate Sugar Cookies recipe for 12–15 minutes. Let cool completely, about 30 minutes.

2   Spoon the filling into a paper cone or pastry bag fitted with a ¼-inch (6-mm) plain round tip (page 15). Turn half of the cookies bottom side up. Pipe a layer of filling over each cookie bottom. Gently press the remaining cookies, bottom side down, onto the filling. Refrigerate until firm, at least 1 hour or up to overnight.

3   Store the cookies in an airtight container, layered between sheets of parchment paper, in the refrigerator for up to 3 days.

All-purpose flour for dusting

Dough for Chocolate Sugar Cookies (page 21), cut into 2-inch (5-cm) hearts

Pink and white sanding sugar for sprinkling (optional)

Vanilla Cream Filling (page 119) or Raspberry Cream Filling (page 119)

TOOLS NEEDED

2-inch heart-shaped cookie cutter; paper cone or pastry bag with a ¼-inch (6-mm) round tip

The jagged pattern imprinted on these cookies is achieved by pressing the serrated end of a cake comb into the dough. This metal or plastic tool is designed to make a pattern in cake frosting.

Orange gel-paste
food coloring (page 11)

Dough for Vanilla Sugar
Cookies (page 18)

All-purpose flour for dusting

4 oz (125 g) white chocolate

Chocolate Glaze (page 116),
warmed

TOOLS NEEDED

Ruler; pizza wheel or
chef's knife; cake comb

CANDY CORN COOKIES

makes about 32 cookies

1   Line 3 baking sheets with parchment paper.

2   Add 1 or 2 drops of food coloring to the dough and knead just until the color is completely distributed. On a lightly floured work surface, using a floured rolling pin, roll the dough to about ¼ inch (6 mm) thick. Using a ruler as a straightedge and a pizza wheel or sharp knife, cut triangles of various sizes. Use a metal spatula to transfer the cookies to the prepared sheets, grouping like-sized shapes and spacing them 1 inch (2.5 cm) apart. Press the dough scraps together, roll out, and cut out additional triangles. Use the largest teeth on a cake comb to firmly press down across each triangle from the base to the tip, spacing the rows of serrations about ¼ inch apart. Avoid cutting completely through the dough. Chill in the refrigerator or freezer until firm, about 15 minutes.

3   Bake the cookies according to the Vanilla Sugar Cookies recipe for 16–19 minutes. Let cool completely, about 30 minutes. Reserve the parchment-lined baking sheets.

4   In a heatproof bowl set over (but not touching) simmering water, heat the white chocolate, stirring frequently, until it has almost completely melted. Remove from the heat and continue to stir until completely melted. Dip the base of each triangle into the glaze and gently shake to let the excess drip off. Dip the tip of the triangle into the white chocolate and gently shake to let the excess drip off. Transfer to the lined sheets. Refrigerate the cookies until the chocolates are set, about 30 minutes.

5   Store the cookies in a single layer in an airtight container in the refrigerator for up to 3 days.

Using cookie cutters in various sizes makes this collection that much more special. When baking the cookies, group similar sizes on a sheet so that they finish at the same time.

TWINKLE STARS
makes 20–30 cookies

Dough for Vanilla Sugar Cookies (page 18), cut into 20 large or 30 small star shapes

Royal Icing (page 116)

White sanding sugar for sprinkling

TOOLS NEEDED

Assorted star-shaped cookie cutters; paper cone or pastry bag with a ¼-inch (6-mm) round tip

1 Bake the cookies according to the Vanilla Sugar Cookies recipe, grouping like-sized cookies together. Smaller cookies should bake for 10–12 minutes and larger ones for 16–19 minutes. Let cool completely, about 30 minutes.

2 Spoon the icing into a paper cone or pastry bag with a ¼-inch (6-mm) round tip (page 15). Pipe the icing around the edge of each cookie to form a border. Then pipe the icing into the middle of the cookie, letting it run to the edges of the border (see illustrations on page 25). Gently tap the cookie twice to settle the icing and set aside to firm up at least 2 hours or overnight. While the icing is still wet, sprinkle with sanding sugar. Let the cookies dry completely, at least 6 hours or up to overnight.

3 Store the cookies in an airtight container, layered between sheets of parchment paper, at room temperature for up to 3 days.

Once the icing has dried completely, it becomes a blank canvas for a painted work of art. If you can find cookie cutters in an assortment of sizes, make a forest of small and large trees.

Dough for Gingerbread Cookies (page 22), cut into trees

Royal Icing (page 116)

¼ teaspoon green powdered food coloring (page 11)

Orange or almond extract

1 teaspoon unsweetened cocoa powder

TOOLS NEEDED

Tree-shaped cookie cutters; paper cone or pastry bag with a ¼-inch (6-mm) round tip; paintbrush

GINGERBREAD TREES

makes about 24 cookies

1   Bake the cookies according to the Gingerbread Cookies recipe for 12–15 minutes. Let cool completely, about 30 minutes.

2   Spoon the icing into a paper cone or pastry bag with a ¼-inch (6-mm) plain round tip (page 15). Pipe the icing around the edge of each cookie to form a border. Pipe the icing into the middle of the cookie, letting it run to the edges of the border (see illustrations on page 25). Gently tap the cookie twice to settle the icing. Set the cookies aside to dry, at least 6 hours or up to overnight.

3   In a small bowl, combine the green food coloring and 1 or 2 drops orange extract. Using a clean small paintbrush, stir until the mixture forms a paste as thick as honey. Brush the mixture on a paper towel or a piece of parchment paper to test the darkness of the color. Using delicate strokes, paint diagonal lines of green on each cookie from the tip of the tree to the trunk, working from both sides of the cookie. Clean the brush. In another small bowl, combine the cocoa powder and 1 or 2 drops extract. Stir with the brush until a thick paste forms. Paint thin vertical lines on the trunk of each tree to simulate bark. Let the cookies dry completely, at least 1 hour.

4   Store the cookies in an airtight container, layered between sheets of parchment paper, at room temperature for up to 3 days.

MODERN CLASSICS

Thin and crispy, these oatmeal cookies will satisfy your sweet tooth with a rich caramel and chocolate flavor. Glaze them the same day they will be served, as they will soften if stored in the refrigerator.

GLAZED OATMEAL LACE COOKIES

makes about 35 cookies

1   In a bowl, whisk together the flour, ½ cup (2 oz/60 g) of the oats, and the salt. In a saucepan, combine the butter, corn syrup, and sugar. Bring to a boil over medium-high heat and cook, stirring occasionally, until the butter has completely melted, about 5 minutes. Pour the hot butter mixture over the oat mixture and add the vanilla. Stir with a wooden spoon until the oat mixture is completely incorporated. Cover and refrigerate the dough for at least 2 hours or up to 3 days.

2   Preheat the oven to 325° (165°C). Line 3 baking sheets with parchment paper or nonstick silicone baking mats.

3   Place the remaining 1 cup (3 oz/90 g) oats in a bowl. Scoop up rounded teaspoons of the dough and roll in the oats, pressing the oats into the dough. Place the cookies on the prepared sheets, spacing them about 3 inches (7.5 cm) apart.

4   Bake until the edges are lightly browned and the tops are lightly golden in the center, 8–10 minutes. Let cool on the sheets for 5 minutes. Using a metal spatula, transfer to wire racks and let cool completely, about 15 minutes. Store the cookies in an airtight container, layered between sheets of parchment paper, at room temperature for up to 2 days.

5   To glaze the cookies, arrange them on wire racks. Using a small spoon, drizzle the chocolate glaze over each cookie, then drizzle the caramel glaze in the opposite direction. Refrigerate the cookies until the glaze is firm, about 20 minutes. Serve right away.

½ cup (2½ oz/75 g) all-purpose flour

1½ cups (5 oz/150 g) rolled oats

¼ teaspoon salt

½ cup (4 oz/125 g) unsalted butter

½ cup (4 fl oz/125 ml) light corn syrup

½ cup (4 oz/125 g) sugar

¼ teaspoon pure vanilla extract

Chocolate Glaze (page 116)

Caramel Glaze (page 117)

TOOLS NEEDED
Small spoon

It's important to let the piped dough stand for 1 hour before baking; otherwise, the tops will crack. Sprinkling the dough with sanding sugar before baking gives these cookies an attractive sparkle.

SPARKLY MACARONS
makes about 35 cookies

1½ cups (6 oz/185 g) confectioner's sugar

1¼ cups (5 oz/140 g) blanched almond flour

3 large egg whites

Pinch salt

¼ cup (2 oz/60 g) granulated sugar

Pink gel-paste food coloring (page 11)

½ teaspoon raspberry extract

White sanding sugar for sprinkling

Vanilla Cream Filling (page 119)

TOOLS NEEDED

Pastry bag with ½-inch (2.5-cm) round tip; small offset spatula

1   Sift the confectioner's sugar into a large bowl. Whisk in the almond flour. In a clean, large bowl, using an electric mixer on medium-high speed, beat the egg whites until they form a dense foam, about 1 minute. Add the salt. Beating continuously, gradually add the granulated sugar. Beat until stiff, glossy peaks form, 3–4 minutes. Add 1 or 2 drops of the food coloring to reach the desired color and the extract. Using a rubber spatula, gently fold the flour mixture into the beaten whites in 3 batches. Continue to fold just until the flour mixture is incorporated and the food coloring is evenly distributed. Be careful not to overmix, or the dough will deflate and become difficult to pipe.

2   Line 3 baking sheets with parchment paper. Spoon the dough into a large pastry bag with a ½-inch (12-mm) round tip (page 15). Pipe the dough onto the prepared sheets in 1½-inch (4-cm) circles, spacing them 1-inch (2.5 cm) apart. Sprinkle with sanding sugar. Let stand at room temperature, uncovered, for 1 hour.

3   Preheat the oven to 325°F (165°C).

4   Bake until the macarons feel firm to the touch but have not taken on any golden color, 12–15 minutes. Let cool completely on the baking sheets.

5   Turn half of the macarons bottom side up. Using a small offset spatula, spread 1 teaspoon of the filling over each macaron bottom. Gently press the remaining macarons, bottom side down, onto the filling. Refrigerate until firm, about 20 minutes.

6   Store the cookies in an airtight container, layered between sheets of parchment paper, in the refrigerator for up to 2 days.

Tart marmalade complements the sweet almond crunch in these cookies. Almond flour can be purchased or use a food processor to finely grind 3 ounces (90 g) of whole almonds.

ALMOND-MARMALADE SPOONPRINTS

makes about 25 cookies

1 Preheat the oven to 350°F (180°C). Line 3 baking sheets with parchment paper.

2 In a bowl, whisk together the 1½ cups all-purpose flour, the almond flour, and the salt. In a large bowl, using an electric mixer on medium-high speed, beat the butter and granulated sugar until light and fluffy, 2–3 minutes. Add the egg yolk and almond extract and beat on low speed until the egg is completely incorporated. Beating on low speed, slowly add the flour mixture and continue to beat until just incorporated, scraping down the sides of the bowl as needed.

3 Shape level tablespoons of the dough into 1-inch (2.5-cm) logs and place on the prepared sheets, spacing them about 1 inch apart. Using the floured handle of a wooden spoon or a floured thumb, make a deep indentation in the center of each cookie. In a small bowl, mix the egg white with 2 teaspoons water. Brush each cookie with the egg white mixture and fill each indentation with 1 rounded teaspoon of marmalade. Press almonds onto the exterior of each cookie and sprinkle with sanding sugar, if using. Bake for 18–20 minutes; until the cookies are light golden around the edges. Let cool on the baking sheets for 5 minutes. Transfer to wire racks and let cool completely, about 30 minutes.

4 Store the cookies in an airtight container, layered between sheets of parchment paper, in the refrigerator for up to 3 days.

1½ cups (7½ oz/235 g) all-purpose flour, plus flour for shaping cookies

½ cup (2 oz/60 g) almond flour

¼ teaspoon salt

¾ cup (6 oz/185 g) unsalted butter, at room temperature

½ cup (4 oz/125 g) granulated sugar

1 large egg yolk, separated

1 teaspoon almond extract

½ cup (5 oz/155 g) blood orange marmalade

½ cup (3 oz/90 g) slivered blanched almonds, toasted

White sanding sugar (optional)

TOOLS NEEDED
Wooden spoon; pastry brush

Eggs will whip with the most volume at room temperature. It's best to separate them cold from the refrigerator and then let them sit out to warm for about 30 minutes before whipping.

1 cup (4 oz/125 g) confectioner's sugar

2 large egg whites, at room temperature

½ teaspoon salt

2 teaspoons pure vanilla extract or other extract, such as peppermint or almond

Unsweetened cocoa powder for dusting (optional)

TOOLS NEEDED

Pastry bag with a ¼-inch (6-mm) round tip

MERINGUE SPIRALS

makes about 20 cookies

1   Preheat the oven to 250°F (120°C). Line 3 large baking sheets with parchment paper. Trace twenty 2 to 3 inch (5 to 7.5 cm) circles on the paper, and then turn the paper over to avoid contact with the ink and batter.

2   Sift the sugar into a bowl. In a clean large bowl, using an electric mixer on medium-high speed, beat the egg whites until foamy, about 1 minute. Add the salt. Continue beating on medium-high speed until a dense foam forms, about 1 minute. Beating continuously, gradually add the sifted sugar, about 2 tablespoons at a time, until the sugar has been incorporated and the mixture is glossy and voluminous, 6–7 minutes. Add the vanilla and mix just until combined, about 1 minute more.

3   Spoon the egg white mixture into a large pastry bag with a ¼-inch (6-mm) round tip (page 15). Pipe the mixture onto the prepared baking sheets, starting in the center of each traced round, and moving in circular motion working your way around to the outside of the traced round spacing 1 inch (2.5 cm) apart. Let stand at room temperature, uncovered, for 30 minutes.

4   Bake until the cookies feel firm and dry, 25–30 minutes. If they still feel tacky, turn off the oven and let them remain in the oven. Transfer to wire racks and let cool completely, about 30 minutes. Dust the cookies evenly with cocoa powder (if using) just before serving.

5   Store the cookies in an airtight container, layered between sheets of parchment paper, in the refrigerator for up to 3 days.

Strong vanilla flavor combined with brown sugar and chocolate is the signature of these rich, moist cookies. The confectioner's sugar coating gives the finished cookies a dramatic look.

CHOCOLATE-BUTTERSCOTCH CRACKLES

makes about 45 cookies

1 In a bowl, whisk together the flour, baking powder, and salt. In a heatproof bowl set over (but not touching) simmering water, heat the chocolate and butter, stirring frequently, until both have melted and the mixture is smooth, about 5 minutes. Remove the bowl from the heat and let cool slightly.

2 Add the brown sugar, eggs, and vanilla seeds and vanilla extract to the chocolate mixture and whisk until just combined, about 1 minute. Add the flour mixture and, using a rubber spatula, mix until just combined, about 1 minute. Cover and refrigerate the dough until well chilled and firm, at least 1 hour or up to overnight.

3 Preheat the oven to 350°F (180°C). Line 3 baking sheets with parchment paper.

4 Place the confectioner's sugar in a bowl. Scoop level tablespoonfuls of dough and roll between the palms of your hands to form balls. Roll the balls in the confectioner's sugar to coat them completely. Place the balls on the prepared sheets, spacing them about 2 inches (5 cm) apart.

5 Bake until the cookies are puffed, have a cracked appearance, and feel firm to the touch around the edges, 12–15 minutes. Let cool on the sheets for 5 minutes. Using a metal spatula, transfer to wire racks and let cool completely, about 30 minutes.

6 Store the cookies in an airtight container, layered between sheets of parchment paper, in the refrigerator for up to 3 days.

2½ cups (12½ oz/390 g) all-purpose flour

1¼ teaspoons baking powder

½ teaspoon salt

4 oz (125 g) unsweetened chocolate, coarsely chopped

½ cup (4 oz/125 g) unsalted butter, at room temperature

2 cups (14 oz/440 g) firmly packed dark brown sugar

2 large eggs

1 vanilla bean, split in half lengthwise and seeds scraped

1 tablespoon pure vanilla extract

½ cup (2 oz/60 g) confectioner's sugar

Chewy and moist on the inside, these indulgent bars get their crunch from toffee pieces mixed into the dough and a generous sprinkling of almonds on top.

2¼ cups (11½ oz/360 g) all-purpose flour

1 teaspoon baking powder

¼ teaspoon salt

1 cup (8 oz/250 g) unsalted butter, at room temperature

1 cup (8 oz/250 g) granulated sugar

1 cup (7 oz/220 g) firmly packed dark brown sugar

2 large eggs

1 teaspoon pure vanilla extract

8 oz (125 g) toffee pieces

¾ cup (3 oz/90 g) almonds, coarsely chopped

TOOLS NEEDED
Large offset spatula; toothpick

CRUNCHY TOFFEE TRIANGLES

makes about 18 cookies

1   Preheat the oven to 350°F (180°C). Butter a 9-by-13-inch (23-by-33-cm) baking pan. Line with parchment paper, letting the paper overhang the long sides by 1 inch (2.5 cm).

2   In a bowl, whisk together the flour, baking powder, and salt. In a large bowl, using an electric mixer on medium-high speed, beat together the butter and sugars until light and fluffy, 2–3 minutes. Add the eggs and vanilla and beat on low speed until the eggs are completely incorporated. Beating on low speed, slowly add the flour mixture and continue to beat until almost incorporated. Add the toffee pieces and beat on low speed until just incorporated, scraping down the sides of the bowl as needed. Use a metal offset spatula to spread the dough evenly in the prepared pan. Sprinkle the top evenly with the almonds.

3   Bake until golden around the edges and a toothpick inserted in the center comes out with only moist crumbs attached, 25–30 minutes. Transfer the pan to a wire rack and let cool completely, about 1 hour. Run a metal spatula around the edges of the pan and use the parchment paper to lift the bar from the pan. Cut into 18 triangles.

4   Store the cookies in an airtight container, layered between sheets of parchment paper, in the refrigerator for up to 4 days.

These tender, buttery cookies can be made up to 1 month in advance and frozen. For a variation, omit the pistachios and add 2 tablespoons molasses after the butter and sugar are combined.

PISTACHIO SABLES

makes about 35 cookies

1 In a bowl, whisk together the 2 cups flour and the salt. In a large bowl, using an electric mixer on medium-high speed, beat together the butter and confectioner's sugar until light and fluffy, 2–3 minutes. Add the egg white and beat on low speed until completely incorporated. Beating on low speed, slowly add the flour mixture and continue to beat until almost incorporated. Add the pistachios and 1 drop food coloring, if using, and beat on low speed until just incorporated, scraping down the sides of the bowl as needed. Using lightly floured hands, form the dough into a 15-inch (38-cm) log about 2 inches (5 cm) in diameter. Sprinkle with the sanding sugar and gently press it into the dough with your hands. Wrap the dough in plastic wrap and refrigerate until firm, at least 1 hour or up to overnight.

2 Preheat the oven to 350°F (180°C). Line 3 baking sheets with parchment paper.

3 Using a chef's knife, cut the dough crosswise into slices about ¼ inch (6 mm) thick. Place the cookies on the prepared sheets, spacing them 1 inch (2.5 cm) apart.

4 Bake until the edges of the cookies feel firm to the touch but have not yet taken on any golden color, 14–17 minutes. Let cool on the sheets for 5 minutes. Using a metal spatula, transfer to wire racks and let cool completely, about 30 minutes.

5 Store the cookies in an airtight container, layered between sheets of parchment paper, in the refrigerator for up to 4 days.

2 cups (10 oz/315 g) all-purpose flour, plus more for dusting

¼ teaspoon salt

1 cup (8 oz/250 g) unsalted butter, at room temperature

1 cup (4 oz/125 g) confectioner's sugar

1 large egg white

½ cup (2 oz/60 g) pistachios, coarsely chopped

Green food coloring (optional)

White sanding sugar for sprinkling

TOOLS NEEDED
Chef's knife

These chocolate waffle cookies are thin and crispy like thin pizza crust. The distinctive pattern comes from baking the cookies in a waffle cone maker. You can also use a traditional pizzelle maker.

5 tablespoons (2½ oz/75 g) unsalted butter

¾ cup (4 oz/125 g) all-purpose flour

⅓ cup (1 oz/30 g) unsweetened cocoa powder

¼ teaspoon salt

2 large eggs

1 cup (8 oz/250 g) sugar

1 teaspoon pure vanilla extract

4 oz (125 g) white chocolate, coarsely chopped

TOOLS NEEDED

Waffle cone maker or pizzelle maker; 3-inch (7.5-cm) round cookie cutter

CHOCOLATE WAFFLE COOKIES
makes about 28 cookies

1   Line 3 large baking sheets with parchment paper.

2   In a small saucepan over medium heat, melt the butter, stirring occasionally. Set aside to cool slightly. In a small bowl, whisk together the flour, cocoa, and salt. In a large bowl, whisk together the eggs and sugar vigorously until the mixture is pale in color and fluffy in texture, about 1 minute. Add the melted butter, flour mixture, and vanilla and whisk until completely incorporated, about 1 minute. Cover and refrigerate the dough until well chilled, at least 1 hour or up to 3 days.

3   Preheat a waffle cone or pizzelle maker following the manufacturer's instructions. For each cookie, place 1½ teaspoons of the dough in the cone maker and cook until the cookie is firm around the edges, about 3 minutes. Use a wide metal spatula to remove the cookie from the waffle maker and immediately while the cookie is still warm, cut using a 3-inch round (7.5-cm) cookie cutter for perfectly smooth sides. (Alternately, omit cutting for a more rustic looking cookie.) Let the cookies cool completely on wire racks. They will become crisp as they cool.

4   In a heatproof bowl set over (but not touching) simmering water, heat the white chocolate, stirring frequently, until almost completely melted. Remove the bowl from the heat and continue to stir until completely melted. Let cool slightly, about 5 minutes. Dip the cookies halfway into the white chocolate and gently shake to remove any excess. Place the cookies on the prepared sheets and refrigerate until firm, at least 15 minutes.

5   Store the cookies in an airtight container, layered between sheets of parchment paper, in the refrigerator for up to 3 days.

These holiday wreaths will make a festive display. Light and crisp in texture and flavored with fresh lemon and herbaceous thyme, they taste as good as they look.

LEMON-THYME WREATHS

makes about 30 cookies

1   In a bowl, whisk together the 2 cups flour, the baking powder, and the salt. In a large bowl, using an electric mixer on medium-high speed, beat the butter, shortening, and granulated sugar until light and fluffy, 2–3 minutes. Add the egg yolk and lemon zest and juice and beat on low speed until the egg is completely incorporated. Beating on low speed, slowly add the flour mixture and continue to beat just until incorporated, scraping down the sides of the bowl as needed. Press the dough into a 7-inch (18-cm) disk. Wrap tightly in plastic wrap and refrigerate until firm, at least 1 hour or up to overnight.

2   Preheat the oven to 325°F (165°C). Line 3 baking sheets with parchment paper. In a small bowl, whisk the egg white with 2 teaspoons water.

3   On a lightly floured work surface, using a floured rolling pin, roll the dough to about ¼ inch (6 mm) thick. Using a 2½-inch (6-cm) round cookie cutter, cut out as many shapes as possible. Use a metal spatula to transfer the cookies to the prepared sheets, spacing them 1 inch (2.5 cm) apart. Use a 1-inch round cookie cutter to cut a small circle from the center of each shape. Press the dough scraps together, roll out, and cut out additional wreaths. Brush each wreath with the reserved egg white mixture and top with the thyme leaves and sanding sugar.

4   Bake until the cookies are lightly golden around the edges, 14–17 minutes. Let cool on the sheets for 5 minutes. Using the spatula, transfer the cookies to wire racks and let cool, about 30 minutes. Spoon the icing into a paper cone with a ⅛-inch (3-mm) round tip (page 15). Pipe dots of icing on each wreath. Let the icing dry completely, about 2 hours.

5   Store the cookies in an airtight container, layered between sheets of parchment paper, in the refrigerator for up to 4 days.

2 cups (10 oz/315 g) all-purpose flour, plus more for dusting

½ teaspoon baking powder

¼ teaspoon salt

½ cup (4 oz/125 g) unsalted butter, at room temperature

½ cup (4 oz/125 g) vegetable shortening

1 cup (8 oz/250 g) granulated sugar

1 large egg, separated

1 tablespoon finely grated lemon zest

2 teaspoons fresh lemon juice

1 bunch fresh thyme, leaves and tips picked

Sanding sugar for sprinkling

Royal Icing (page 116)

TOOLS NEEDED

Paper cone with a ⅛-inch (3-mm) round tip; 2½-inch (6-cm) and 1-inch (2.5-cm) round cookie cutters

These coconut macaroons have a crisp exterior and a soft, chewy center. For an interesting variation, fold 1 tablespoon finely grated lime zest into the beaten whites with the shredded coconut.

CHOCOLATE-DIPPED COCONUT CLOUDS
makes about 25 cookies

Nonstick cooking spray

3 large egg whites, at room temperature

¼ teaspoon cream of tartar

Pinch salt

¾ cup (6 oz/185 g) sugar

½ teaspoon pure vanilla extract

4½ cups (10 oz/150 g) sweetened shredded coconut

Chocolate Glaze (page 116)

1   Preheat the oven to 325°F (165°C). Line 3 baking sheets with parchment paper and lightly spray the paper with nonstick cooking spray.

2   In a clean large bowl, combine the egg whites and cream of tartar. Using a mixer on medium-high speed, beat until the egg whites form a dense foam, about 1 minute. Add the salt. Beating continuously, gradually add the sugar and beat until stiff peaks form, 3–4 minutes. Using a rubber spatula, stir in the vanilla. In 3 batches, gently fold the coconut into the beaten whites, folding just until the coconut is incorporated. Place rounded tablespoonfuls of the dough on the prepared sheets, spacing them 1 inch (2.5 cm) apart.

3   Bake until the edges begin to turn lightly golden brown, 19–22 minutes. Let cool completely on the sheets, about 30 minutes. Dip the bottom of each cookie in the glaze and return to a parchment-lined sheet. Refrigerate until the glaze is set, about 10 minutes.

4   Store the cookies, in a single layer, in an airtight container at room temperature for up to 4 days.

Traditionally baked two times, biscotti are crisp and dry, perfectly suited for dunking in espresso or dessert wine. They remain fresh long enough to package and send to friends and family as gifts.

APRICOT-PISTACHIO BISCOTTI

makes about 45 cookies

1 Preheat the oven to 350°F (180°C). Line a baking sheet with parchment paper. In a small bowl, whisk the egg white with 1 teaspoon water; set aside.

2 In a bowl, whisk together the flour, baking powder, and salt. In a large bowl, using an electric mixer on medium-high speed, beat the butter and granulated sugar until light and fluffy, about 2 minutes. Add the 2 eggs and almond and vanilla extracts and beat on low speed until the eggs are incorporated. Beating on low speed, slowly add the flour mixture and continue to beat until almost fully incorporated, scraping down the sides of the bowl as needed. Add the pistachios and apricots and beat on low speed just until distributed.

3 Divide the dough in half. Shape each piece into a 9½-by-1½-inch (24-by-4-cm) square log and transfer the logs to the prepared baking sheet, spacing them 4 inches (10 cm) apart. Brush the logs with the egg white mixture and sprinkle with the sanding sugar.

4 Bake until the edges of the biscotti are light brown and the tops feel firm, 20–24 minutes. Remove the cookies and leave the oven on. Transfer the sheet to a wire rack and let cool slightly, about 20 minutes. Using a serrated knife, cut each log into 22 slices about ½ inch (12 mm) thick. Arrange the slices, cut side down, on the sheet and bake until the biscotti are golden brown and completely dry, 10–12 minutes. Using a metal spatula, transfer the biscotti to a wire rack and let cool completely.

5 Store the cookies in an airtight container, layered between sheets of parchment paper, in the refrigerator for up to 1 week.

---

2 large eggs, plus 1 large egg white

2 cups (10 oz/315 g) all-purpose flour

1 teaspoon baking powder

¼ teaspoon salt

4 tablespoons (2 oz/60 g) unsalted butter, at room temperature

¾ cup (2 oz/60 g) granulated sugar

1 teaspoon almond extract

½ teaspoon pure vanilla extract

½ cup (2 oz/60 g) unsalted, roasted pistachio nuts, coarsely chopped

½ cup (4 oz/125 g) packed dried apricots, coarsely chopped

¼ cup (2 oz/60 g) sanding sugar or granulated sugar for sprinkling

TOOLS NEEDED

Serrated knife

2¼ cups (11½ oz/360 g) all-purpose flour

½ teaspoon salt

¾ cup (6 oz/185 g) plus 2 tablespoons unsalted butter, at room temperature

1 cup (4 oz/125 g) confectioner's sugar

1 large egg, at room temperature

1 teaspoon pure vanilla extract

Chocolate Glaze (page 116), chilled

TOOLS NEEDED

1 pastry bag with a ¾-inch (2-cm) star tip and one pastry bag with a ¼-inch (6-mm) round tip

Be sure that the ingredients for the dough are at room temperature, as the dough needs to be soft enough to extrude easily from the pastry tip. The cookies can also be shaped with a cookie press.

VANILLA SPRITZ SANDWICHES

makes about 15 cookies

1   Have ready 3 baking sheets.

2   In a bowl, whisk together the flour and salt. In a large bowl, using an electric mixer on medium-high speed, beat the butter and sugar until light and fluffy, 2–3 minutes. Add the egg and vanilla and beat on low speed until the egg is completely incorporated. Beating on low speed, slowly add the flour mixture and continue to beat until just incorporated, scraping down the sides of the bowl as needed. Transfer the dough to a large pastry bag fitted with a ¾-inch (2-cm) open star tip (page 15).

3   Pipe rosettes of dough onto the sheets, using firm pressure to extrude the dough in a circular motion. Make cookies about 1¼ inches (3 cm) in diameter, spacing them 1 inch (2.5 cm) apart. Chill in the refrigerator or freezer until firm, about 15 minutes.

4   Preheat the oven to 325°F (165°C).

5   Bake until the cookies are firm to the touch but have not yet taken on any golden color, 15–17 minutes. Let cool on the sheets for 5 minutes. Using a metal spatula, transfer to wire racks and let cool completely, about 30 minutes.

6   Spoon the glaze into a pastry bag with a ¼-inch (6-mm) round tip. Turn half of the cookies bottom side up. Pipe a layer of glaze over each cookie bottom. Gently press the remaining cookies, bottom side down, onto the filling. Refrigerate until firm, about 1 hour.

7   Store the cookies in an airtight container, layered between sheets of parchment paper, in the refrigerator for up to 3 days.

These cookies are reminiscent of brownies in texture. With the addition of dark chocolate icing and candied orange peel, they are elevated to the kind of dessert served in a fine restaurant.

ORANGE TRUFFLE COOKIES

makes about 40 cookies

1   In a bowl, whisk together the ½ cup flour, the cocoa, baking soda, and salt. Place about three-fourths of the chocolate and the butter in a heatproof bowl set over (but not touching) barely simmering water. Heat, stirring frequently, until the chocolate is completely melted and smooth, 4–5 minutes. Remove the bowl from the heat and let cool to lukewarm, about 15 minutes.

2   In a large bowl, using an electric mixer on medium-high speed, beat together the eggs and sugar until pale and thick, about 2 minutes. Add the orange extract and beat to combine. Add the melted chocolate and, using a rubber spatula, gently stir to combine. Using the spatula, gently stir in the flour mixture in 2 batches just until incorporated. Add the remaining chopped chocolate and stir just until incorporated. Cover and refrigerate the dough until well chilled, at least 1 hour or up to overnight.

3   Preheat the oven to 350°F (180°C). Line 3 baking sheets with parchment paper.

4   Scoop up rounded teaspoonfuls of the dough and, using floured hands, roll into balls. Place on the prepared sheets, spaced about 1 inch (2.5 cm) apart. Bake until the cookies feel firm in the center but have not yet taken on additional color, 10–12 minutes. Let cool on the sheets for 5 minutes. Using a metal spatula, transfer the cookies to wire racks to cool completely, about 30 minutes.

5   Spoon the filling into a pastry bag fitted with a ½-inch (12-mm) rose petal tip (page 15). Pipe 2 rows of filling in a zigzag pattern down the center of each cookie. Place 1 candied orange curl on each cookie just before serving. Store the cookies in a single layer in an airtight container at room temperature for up to 3 days.

½ cup (2½ oz/75 g) all-purpose flour, plus more for dusting

¼ cup (¾ oz/20 g) unsweetened cocoa powder

¼ teaspoon baking soda

¼ teaspoon salt

8 oz (250 g) bittersweet chocolate, coarsely chopped

6 tablespoons (3 oz/90 g) unsalted butter, cut into pieces

2 large eggs, at room temperature

¾ cup (6 oz/185 g) sugar

1 teaspoon orange extract

Dark Chocolate Cream Filling (page 119)

Candied Orange Curls (page 121)

TOOLS NEEDED

Pastry bag with a ½-inch (12-mm) rose petal tip

Graham flour, found in specialty-food stores, is a type of whole wheat flour used to make the crackers that many people remember from their childhood.

1 cup (5 oz/155 g) all-purpose flour, plus flour for dusting

¾ cup (5 oz/145 g) graham flour

1 teaspoon baking powder

¾ teaspoon ground cinnamon

¼ teaspoon salt

6 tablespoons (3 oz/90 g) unsalted butter, at room temperature

⅓ cup (2½ oz/75 g) firmly packed dark brown sugar

⅓ cup (1½ oz/45 g) confectioner's sugar

1 large egg plus 1 large egg yolk

1 tablespoon pale clover honey

Cream Cheese Filling (page 118)

TOOLS NEEDED

2½-inch (6-cm) round fluted cookie cutter; paring knife; 3 paper cones with ¼-inch (6-mm) round tips

GRAHAM CRACKER SANDWICHES
makes about 25 cookies

1   Preheat the oven to 325°F (165°C). Line 3 baking sheets with parchment paper. In a bowl, whisk together the flours, baking powder, cinnamon, and salt. In a large bowl, using an electric mixer on medium-high speed, beat together the butter and sugars until light and fluffy, 2—3 minutes. Add the whole egg, egg yolk, and honey and beat until the eggs are completely incorporated. Beating on low speed, slowly add the flour mixture and continue to beat until just incorporated, scraping down the sides of the bowl as needed.

2   Transfer the dough onto a floured work surface. Using a floured rolling pin, roll the dough to about ¼ inch (6 mm) thick. Using a 2½-inch (6-cm) round fluted cutter, cut out shapes. In half of the cookies, use the tip of a paring knife to cut a 1½-by-⅛-inch (4-cm-by-3-mm) window in the center. Then cut a 1-by-⅛-inch (2.5-cm-by-3-mm) window just above and just below the center window. Use a metal spatula to transfer the cookies to the prepared sheets, spacing them 1 inch apart. Bake until the cookies are golden around the edges, 15—18 minutes.

3   Let cool on the sheets for 5 minutes, then transfer to wire racks to cool completely, about 30 minutes. Turn the cooled solid cookies bottom side up. Transfer each of the three fillings into paper cones with ¼-inch round tips (page 15). Pipe a wide strip of each filling onto the bottom of each solid cookie. Press the remaining cookies, bottom side down, onto the filling, lining up each open space over a different filling.

4   Store the cookies in an airtight container, layered between sheets of parchment paper, in the refrigerator for up to 3 days.

When you first try these chocolate cookies, prepare for an unexpected sweet and salty twist. For an even more decadent variation, dip the cookies in Caramel Glaze (page 117) after baking.

CHOCOLATE PRETZELS

makes about 25 cookies

1   Preheat the oven to 325°F (165°C). Line 3 baking sheets with parchment paper. In a small bowl, whisk the egg white with 2 teaspoons water until blended. Set aside.

2   In a bowl, whisk together the flour and cocoa powder. In a large bowl, using an electric mixer on medium-high speed, beat the butter and confectioner's sugar until light and fluffy, about 2 minutes. Add the egg yolk and beat on low speed until completely incorporated. Beating on low speed, slowly add the flour mixture and continue to beat until almost fully incorporated, scraping down the sides of the bowl as needed. Add the cream and beat just until combined.

3   For each cookie, shape 1 level tablespoon of dough into a round ball. Using the palms of both hands, roll the ball, using a back and forth motion, into an 11-inch (28-cm) rope. Arrange the rope in a U shape on the work surface. Holding the ends of the rope, place one end over the other, then bring the ends toward you and lay them on top of the curved portion of the U. (The shaped cookies can be wrapped well in plastic wrap and frozen for up to 1 month.) Using a pastry brush, brush each cookie with the egg white mixture and sprinkle generously with sanding sugar and sparingly with sea salt.

4   Bake until the cookies feel firm to the touch in the center, but have not taken on additional color, 17–20 minutes. Let cool on the sheets for 5 minutes. Using a metal spatula, transfer to wire racks and let cool completely, about 30 minutes.

5   Store the cookies in an airtight container, layered between sheets of parchment paper, at room temperature for up to 3 days.

1 large egg, separated

1¾ cups (9 oz/280 g) all-purpose flour

⅓ cup (1 oz/30 g) cocoa powder

¾ cup (6 oz/185 g) unsalted butter, at room temperature

½ cup (2 oz/60 g) confectioner's sugar

1 tablespoon heavy cream

White sanding sugar for sprinkling

Flaked sea salt for sprinkling

TOOLS NEEDED

Pastry brush

These crisp cookies are delicious on their own. You can also fill the rolled cookies by piping Vanilla Cream Filling (page 119) into them; refrigerate for 20 minutes before serving.

¾ cup (4 oz/125 g) all-purpose flour

¼ teaspoon salt

½ cup (4 oz/125 g) unsalted butter, at room temperature

½ cup (4 oz/125 g) plus 1 tablespoon sugar

3 large egg whites

¾ teaspoon peppermint extract

Gel-paste food coloring in shades of red and brown (page 11)

TOOLS NEEDED

4 pastry bags with ⅛-inch (3-mm) round tips; small offset spatula; chopstick

PEPPERMINT STICKS
makes about 24 cookies

1 In a bowl, whisk together the flour and salt. In a large bowl, using an electric mixer on medium-high speed, beat the butter and sugar until light and fluffy, 2–3 minutes. Add the egg whites and peppermint extract and beat on low speed until the egg is completely incorporated. Beating on low speed, slowly add the flour mixture and continue to beat until just incorporated, scraping down the sides of the bowl as needed.

2 Place 2 tablespoons of the dough into each of 4 small bowls. Color each a different shade of red, starting with pale pink and ending with dark burgundy. To make burgundy, use the tip of a toothpick to add a tiny bit of brown to deep red. Spoon the doughs into separate pastry bags, each with a ⅛-inch (3-mm) round tip (page 15). Refrigerate the dough until chilled, about 30 minutes.

3 Preheat the oven to 325°F (165°C). Line 3 baking sheets with parchment paper. To form each cookie, use a small offset spatula to spread 2 teaspoons of the uncolored dough on the prepared sheets into a 3½-by-4½-inch (9-by-11.5-cm) rectangle about ⅛ inch thick. Pipe a diagonal line of red dough over the rectangle from one side to the opposite side. Continue to pipe lines, using different colors of red and varying the width of the lines. Space the lines ¾ inch (2 cm) apart.

4 Bake until the edges are firm to the touch but have not yet taken on any golden color, 15–17 minutes. Immediately use a metal spatula to remove each cookie from the sheets and invert it onto a work surface. Roll the cookie around a chopstick, then remove the chopstick. Transfer to wire racks and let cool completely, about 15 minutes. If the cookies become too cool and fragile, return them to the oven for 1 minute to soften. Store the cookies in an airtight container for up to 2 days.

In this modern take on the chocolate chip cookie, chocolate pearls replace chips and add a distinctive crunch. Look for the pearls in specialty-food or gourmet markets.

CHOCOLATE CHIP WAFERS

makes about 30 cookies

1 Preheat the oven to 350°F (180°C). Line 3 baking sheets with parchment paper.

2 In a bowl, whisk together the flour, baking soda, and salt. In a large bowl, using an electric mixer on medium-high speed, beat together the butter and sugar until light and fluffy, about 3 minutes. Add the egg and vanilla and beat on low speed until the egg is completely incorporated. Beating on low speed, slowly add the flour mixture and continue to beat until just incorporated, scraping down the sides of the bowl as needed.

3 Using a small offset spatula, evenly spread 1 rounded teaspoonful of dough on a prepared sheet into a 3-by-2-inch (7.5-by-5-cm) rectangle about ⅛ inch (3 mm) thick. Use a metal spatula to drag and scrape the dough so that the corners of the rectangle are square. Arrange chocolate pearls on top of the dough in a pattern. Repeat with the remaining dough, spacing the cookies 1 inch (2.5 cm) apart.

4 Bake until the edges are golden brown, but the tops have not yet taken on additional color, 12–15 minutes. Let cool on the sheets for 5 minutes. Using the metal spatula, transfer the cookies to a cutting board. Using a chef's knife, trim the edges of each cookie into a perfect rectangle. Transfer to wire racks and let cool completely, about 30 minutes.

5 Store the cookies in an airtight container, layered between sheets of parchment paper, at room temperature for up to 4 days.

1½ cups (7½ oz/235 g) all-purpose flour

½ teaspoon baking soda

¼ teaspoon salt

½ cup (4 oz/125 g) plus 2 tablespoons unsalted butter, at room temperature

1 cup (7 oz/220 g) firmly packed dark brown sugar

1 large egg

½ teaspoon pure vanilla extract

1 cup (7 oz/200 g) dark chocolate pearls (¼ inch/6 mm)

TOOLS NEEDED
Chef's knife

2¼ cups (11½ oz/360 g) all-purpose flour

¼ teaspoon salt

1 cup (8 oz/250 g) unsalted butter, at room temperature

1½ cups (12 oz/375 g) sugar

1½ teaspoons pure vanilla extract

1 cup (6 oz/185 g) dried cherries, coarsely chopped

TOOLS NEEDED

10-inch (25-cm) tart pan with a removable bottom; chef's knife

This shortbread is studded with cherries to add extra flavor and texture. If the cherries feel too firm, soften them in 2 tablespoons boiling water for about 10 minutes; they will absorb the liquid.

DRIED CHERRY SHORTBREAD
makes about 30 cookies

1   Preheat the oven to 350°F (180°C). Have ready a 10-inch (25-cm) tart pan with a removable bottom.

2   In a bowl, whisk together the flour and salt. In a large bowl, using an electric mixer on medium-high speed, beat together the butter and 1¼ cups (10 oz/315 g) of the sugar until light and fluffy, 2–3 minutes. Beating on low speed, slowly add the flour mixture, beating until almost incorporated. Add the vanilla and dried cherries and beat on low speed just until the dough forms large clumps and pulls away from the sides of the bowl. Using your hands, evenly press the dough into the tart pan. With a fork, prick the entire surface, making holes ¼ inch (6 mm) deep at 1-inch (2.5-cm) intervals.

3   Place the pan on a baking sheet and bake until the center is very lightly golden brown, 30–35 minutes. Immediately sprinkle the remaining ¼ cup (2 oz/60 g) sugar evenly over the shortbread and use a sharp chef's knife to cut it into squares. Let cool in the pan, about 30 minutes.

4   Remove the cookies from the pan and store in an airtight container, layered between sheets of parchment paper, at room temperature for up to 4 days.

Crunchy in texture from cornmeal, the cookies have a subtle citrus flavor from the addition of lime zest. The dough can be wrapped well and frozen for up to 1 month.

CORNMEAL STICKS

makes about 25 cookies

1   In a bowl, whisk together the flour, the 3 tablespoons cornmeal, and the salt. In a large bowl, using an electric mixer on medium-high speed, beat together the butter and confectioner's sugar until light and fluffy, 2–3 minutes. Beating on low speed, slowly add the flour mixture and continue to beat until almost incorporated, scraping down the sides of the bowl as needed. Add the walnuts, currants, raisins, and lime zest, and beat on low speed until just incorporated.

2   Form the dough into a log about 5 inches (13 cm) wide, 1¼ inches (3 cm) high, and 7 inches (18 cm) long. Sprinkle the ¼ cup cornmeal onto the log, using your hands to gently press it into the dough. Wrap the log tightly in plastic wrap and refrigerate for at least 1 hour or up to overnight.

3   Preheat the oven to 350°F (180°C). Line 3 baking sheets with parchment paper.

4   Use a chef's knife to cut the log crosswise into slices ¼ inch (6 mm) thick. Transfer the cookies to the prepared sheets, spacing them 1 inch (2.5 cm) apart. Sprinkle with the sanding sugar.

5   Bake until the edges turn light golden brown but the centers are barely colored, 16–18 minutes. Let cool on the sheets for 5 minutes. Using a metal spatula, transfer the cookies to wire racks and let cool completely, about 30 minutes.

6   Store the cookies in an airtight container, layered between sheets of parchment paper, at room temperature for up to 4 days.

2¼ cups (11½ oz/360 g) all-purpose flour

3 tablespoons medium-grind yellow cornmeal, plus ¼ cup (1 oz/30 g)

½ teaspoon salt

1 cup (8 oz/250 g) unsalted butter, at room temperature

1 cup (4 oz/125 g) confectioner's sugar

½ cup (2 oz/30 g) walnuts, toasted and coarsely chopped

¼ cup (1½ oz/45 g) currants

½ cup (3 oz/90 g) golden raisins

2 teaspoons finely grated lime zest

White sanding sugar for sprinkling

TOOLS NEEDED
Chef's knife

These crunchy peanut butter cookies are coated in a rich dark chocolate glaze. Best served chilled from the refrigerator, the cookies beg for an accompanying glass of cold milk.

1½ cups (7½ oz/235 g) all-purpose flour, plus flour for dusting

½ teaspoon baking powder

½ teaspoon baking soda

½ teaspoon salt

½ cup (4 oz/125 g) unsalted butter, at room temperature

½ cup (3½ oz/105 g) firmly packed light brown sugar

½ cup (4 oz/125 g) granulated sugar

1 large egg

½ teaspoon pure vanilla extract

1 cup (10 oz/315 g) natural creamy peanut butter

Chocolate Glaze (page 116)

TOOLS NEEDED
Ruler; pizza wheel or paring knife

CHOCOLATE–PEANUT BUTTER SQUARES
makes about 35 cookies

1   In a large bowl, whisk together the 1½ cups flour, the baking powder, baking soda, and salt. In another large bowl, using an electric mixer on medium-high speed, beat the butter and sugars until light and fluffy, 2–3 minutes. Add the egg and vanilla and beat on low speed until the egg is incorporated. Add the peanut butter and beat on low speed just until incorporated. Beating on low speed, slowly add the flour mixture and continue to beat until just incorporated, scraping down the sides of the bowl as needed. Using floured hands, form the dough into a flattened rectangle, wrap in plastic wrap, and refrigerate until firm, at least 1 hour or up to overnight.

2   Preheat the oven to 350°F (180°C). Line 3 baking sheets with parchment paper. On a lightly floured surface, using a floured rolling pin, roll the dough into a 15-by-11-inch (38-by-28-cm) rectangle about ¼ inch (6 mm) thick. Using a ruler as a straightedge and a pizza wheel or sharp paring knife, trim the rectangle to 14 by 10 inches (35 by 25 cm). Cut out thirty-five 2-inch (5-cm) squares. Use a metal spatula to transfer the cookies to the prepared sheets, spacing them 1 inch (2.5 cm) apart.

3   Bake until the cookies are light golden brown around the edges, 15–18 minutes. Let cool on the sheets for 5 minutes. Using the metal spatula, transfer to wire racks and let cool completely, about 30 minutes. Reserve the parchment-lined sheets.

4   Using 2 forks to hold each cookie, dip into the glaze, gently shaking to remove any excess. Transfer to the baking sheets and refrigerate until the glaze is set, about 30 minutes. Dip a paring knife in hot water and wipe dry. Score a crosshatch pattern on each cookie. Wipe the knife clean and dip it in hot water before making the next mark. Store the cookies in an airtight container in the refrigerator for up to 3 days.

If you like cookies for breakfast, this is the recipe for you. These cinnamon-scented wedges taste like the top of a decadent coffee cake. The streusel couldn't be simpler to prepare.

MAPLE-PECAN STREUSEL BARS
makes 18 bars

1   Preheat the oven to 350°F (180°C). Butter a 9-by-13-inch (23-by-33-cm) baking pan. Line with parchment paper, leaving a 1-inch (2.5-cm) overhang on the long sides.

2   In a large bowl, whisk together the flour, cinnamon, salt, and pecans. In a large bowl, using an electric mixer on medium-high speed, beat together the 1 cup butter, the brown sugar, and the confectioner's sugar until light and fluffy, about 2 minutes. Beating on low speed, add the flour mixture and maple extract and continue to beat just until incorporated. The mixture should resemble coarse crumbs.

3   Transfer 3 cups of the dough to the prepared pan. Cover with a sheet of parchment paper. Using the bottom of a measuring cup, press the dough evenly into the pan, lifting the parchment occasionally to make sure that it doesn't stick. The dough should be firmly packed, without holes or cracks. Cover evenly with the remaining dough, sprinkling it over the top and squeezing some of the dough to form large clumps.

4   Bake until lightly golden, 16–18 minutes. Transfer the pan to a wire rack and let cool completely, about 1 hour. Run a metal spatula around the edges of the pan. Drizzle with the glaze and let set for at least 10 minutes. Using a chef's knife, cut into 18 bars.

5   Store the bars in an airtight container, layered between sheets of parchment paper, at room temperature for up to 3 days.

2½ cups (12½ oz/390 g) all-purpose flour

1 teaspoon ground cinnamon

½ teaspoon salt

1½ cups (6 oz/185 g) pecans, finely chopped

1 cup (8 oz/250 g) unsalted butter, at room temperature, plus more for coating

½ cup (3½ oz/105 g) firmly packed light brown sugar

½ cup (2 oz/60 g) confectioner's sugar

2 teaspoons maple extract

Vanilla Glaze (page 117)

TOOLS NEEDED
9-by-13-inch (23-by-33-cm) baking pan; chef's knife

4 cups (1 lb/500 g)
confectioner's sugar

3 tablespoons
meringue powder

½ teaspoon extract such as
vanilla or almond (optional)

ROYAL ICING
makes about 3 cups (24 fl oz/750 ml)

1   In a large bowl, combine the sugar, the meringue powder, ½ cup
(4 fl oz/125 ml) warm water, and the extract, if using. Using an electric
mixer on medium speed, beat until the mixture is fluffy, yet dense,
7–8 minutes.

2   To thin the icing, use a rubber spatula to stir in additional warm water,
1 teaspoon at a time. To test the consistency, drizzle a spoonful of icing into
the bowl; a ribbon should remain on the surface for about 5 seconds.

3   Cover and store in the refrigerator for up to 1 week. Stir vigorously just
before using.

½ cup (4 fl oz/125 ml)
heavy cream

1½ tablespoons
unsalted butter

6 oz (185 g) semisweet
chocolate, finely chopped

Pinch salt

CHOCOLATE GLAZE
makes about 1 cup (8 fl oz/250 ml)

1   In a small saucepan over medium-high heat, bring the cream and
butter to a boil. Remove from the heat. Add the chocolate and salt
and stir to completely cover the chocolate with cream. Let stand for
about 1 minute. Slowly whisk the mixture until it is smooth. Transfer
to a small bowl and let cool, stirring frequently, until the glaze is thick
enough to coat the back of a spoon, 40–45 minutes. (If the glaze
becomes too thick, place in a heatproof bowl over simmering water
in a saucepan and stir until it reaches the right consistency.)

2   Cover and store in the refrigerator for up to 3 days. Bring to room
temperature or warm slightly before using.

VANILLA GLAZE

makes about ½ cup (4 fl oz / 125 ml)

1 cup (4 oz/125 g)
confectioner's sugar

4 teaspoons milk

1 teaspoon pure
vanilla extract

1 Sift the sugar into a bowl. Add the milk and vanilla and stir until completely smooth, about 1 minute.

2 Cover and store in the refrigerator for up to 3 days. Bring to room temperature or warm slightly before using.

CARAMEL GLAZE

makes about 1½ cups (12 fl oz / 375 ml)

1 cup (8 oz/250 g) sugar

½ cup (4 fl oz/125 ml)
heavy cream

Pinch salt

1 In a heavy, high-sided saucepan over medium-high heat, cook the sugar until it begins to melt around the edges, about 4 minutes. Continue to cook, stirring constantly with a wooden spoon, until the sugar is completely melted and turns golden amber, about 2 minutes longer.

2 Carefully pour the cream down the side of the pan in a slow, steady stream (it will bubble and spatter), stirring constantly until the mixture is completely smooth. Stir in the salt. Pour the glaze into a small heatproof bowl and let cool slightly before using, about 20 minutes.

3 Cover and store in the refrigerator for up to 3 days. Bring to room temperature or warm slightly before using.

3 large egg yolks

¼ cup (2 oz/60 g) sugar

¼ cup (3 oz/90 g) pale
clover honey

¾ cup (6 oz/185 g) unsalted
butter, at room temperature

1 teaspoon finely grated
lemon zest

⅛ teaspoon salt

HONEY CREAM FILLING
makes about 1½ cups (12 fl oz/375 ml)

1   In a bowl, using an electric mixer on medium speed, beat the egg yolks
    until fluffy, about 2 minutes. In a small saucepan over medium-high heat,
    bring the sugar, honey, and ¼ cup (2 fl oz/60 ml) water to a boil. Cook
    until the syrup reaches 239°F (115°C) on a candy thermometer.

2   Continuously beating the egg yolks on medium speed, slowly pour the
    hot sugar syrup down the side of the bowl onto the yolks. Beat until
    the mixture is cool and thick, about 5 minutes. Add the butter, lemon zest,
    and salt and beat on medium speed until combined, about 2 minutes.

3   Use the filling immediately or refrigerate overnight. Let the chilled filling
    soften to room temperature, at least 1 hour before using.

⅓ cup (1½ oz/45 g)
confectioner's sugar

1 cup (8 oz/250 g) cream
cheese, at room temperature

2 oz (60 g) unsalted butter,
at room temperature

½ teaspoon pure
vanilla extract

CREAM CHEESE FILLING
makes about 1½ cups (12 fl oz/375 ml)

1   Sift the sugar into a large bowl. Add the cream cheese and butter and,
    using an electric mixer on medium-high speed, beat until the mixture
    is light and fluffy, 2–3 minutes. Add the vanilla and continue to beat on
    low speed until completely combined.

2   Use the filling immediately or refrigerate overnight.

VANILLA CREAM FILLING

makes about 1½ cups (12 fl oz/375 ml)

3/4 cup (6 oz/185 g)
confectioner's sugar

1 cup (8 oz/250 g) unsalted
butter, at room temperature

1½ teaspoons pure
vanilla extract

Pinch salt

1   Sift the sugar into a large bowl and add the butter. Using an electric mixer on low speed, beat until combined. Increase the speed to medium-high and beat until light and fluffy, about 3 minutes. Add the vanilla and salt and beat on low speed just until combined.

2   Store in the refrigerator for up to 3 days. Bring to room temperature before using.

DARK CHOCOLATE VARIATION

In a heatproof bowl set over (but not touching) simmering water, heat 3 oz (90 g) unsweetened chocolate, stirring frequently, until completely melted, about 4 minutes; set aside to cool completely. Add the chocolate to the beaten butter and sugar mixture and beat on low speed until just combined. Refrigerate until firm, about 30 minutes.

RASPBERRY VARIATION

Omit the vanilla extract and add ¼ cup (2 fl oz/60 ml) strained raspberry preserves. If desired, add a small drop of red food coloring.

2 lemons

4 large egg yolks

⅔ cup (5 oz/155 g) sugar

Pinch salt

5 tablespoons (2½ oz/75 g)
unsalted butter, cut into pieces

LEMON CURD

makes 1 cup (8 fl oz/250 ml)

1 Finely grate the zest from the lemons. Cut the lemons in half and squeeze enough juice to measure ⅓ cup (3 fl oz/80 ml).

2 In a heavy-bottomed nonreactive saucepan, whisk together the egg yolks, lemon zest and juice, sugar, and salt. Cook over medium-high heat, whisking constantly and scraping the sides of the pan, until the curd is thick enough to coat the back of a spoon, 5–8 minutes. Do not let the curd boil, or it may turn lumpy.

3 Remove the saucepan from the heat. Whisk in the butter, one piece at a time, until the curd is smooth. Strain through a fine-mesh sieve into a bowl. Cover with plastic wrap, pressing it directly onto the surface of the curd to prevent a skin from forming.

4 Refrigerate until chilled and set, at least 1 hour or up to 3 days.

CANDIED ORANGE CURLS

makes about 45 curls

2 large, firm oranges
3 cups (1½ lb/750 g) sugar

1   Using a vegetable peeler, remove strips of peel from each orange, working from one end to the other. Do not remove too much of the bitter white pith along with the peel. Reserve the orange flesh for another use. Use a knife to cut the peel into strips about 2 inches (5 cm) long and ⅛ inch (3 mm) wide.

2   Bring a saucepan of water to a boil. Add the orange peel strips and boil for 3 minutes. Drain and rinse under cold running water.

3   In a saucepan, combine 2 cups (1 lb/500 g) of the sugar, 2 cups (16 fl oz/500 ml) water, and the orange peel strips. Bring to a simmer over medium-low heat and cook until the strips are soft and translucent, about 30 minutes. Let cool to room temperature in the sugar syrup.

4   Using a slotted spoon, transfer the strips to a wire rack set over a rimmed baking sheet; reserve the syrup for another use. Let stand until the strips feel tacky to the touch, about 1 hour.

5   Spread the remaining 1 cup (8 oz/250 g) sugar in a shallow dish. Toss a handful of the strips in the sugar until completely coated. Wrap the sugar-coated strips around a long wooden skewer and set the skewer across the edges of the baking sheet so that the strips hang from the skewer as they dry. Repeat with the remaining strips. Let the strips dry for at least 1 hour.

6   Store in an airtight container at room temperature for up to 1 week.

Confectioner's sugar for dusting

Brown gel-paste food coloring (page 11)

7 oz (220 g) marzipan

Chocolate Glaze (page 116)

MARZIPAN BARK
makes 24 strips

1   Dust 1 large piece of parchment paper with the sugar.

2   Add 1 to 2 drops of the food coloring to the marzipan and knead until the color is evenly distributed.

3   On the parchment, roll the marzipan into a 12-by-7-inch (30-by-18-cm) rectangle about ⅛ inch (3mm) thick. Using a large offset spatula, evenly spread 1 cup (8 fl oz/250 ml) of the glaze on the marzipan in a ¼-inch (6-mm) layer. Slide the parchment paper onto a baking sheet and refrigerate until the chocolate is set, about 30 minutes.

4   Use a cake comb to drag a bark pattern through the glaze. Refrigerate until very firm, about 1 hour. Using a ruler as a straightedge and a pizza wheel or sharp knife, cut the chocolate marzipan bark into 24 strips, each 7 inches long and ½ inch wide.

5   Use right away or store in an airtight container at room temperature for up to 1 week.

MARZIPAN ROSES

makes 24 small roses

1 Line a baking sheet with parchment paper.

2 Use the tip of a toothpick to add a very small amount of food coloring to the marzipan. Knead until the color is evenly distributed.

3 Form 1 rounded teaspoonful of marzipan into a ball. Roll the marzipan into a 3-inch (7.5-cm) rope and cut into 8 equal pieces, then roll each piece into a ball. Cover the balls with plastic wrap. Dip your fingers in the sugar and press 1 marzipan ball between your thumb and forefinger, pressing the front edge until it is very thin and leaving the back edge rather thick. The thin edge should be jagged and rough, and should curl slightly downward. Transfer the formed petal to the prepared sheet and loosely drape with plastic wrap. Repeat to form the remaining 7 petals.

4 To create a rose, pick up 1 petal, holding the thicker end in your fingertips, and curl the petal inward by rolling it into a loose cigar shape. The thin, ragged edge of the petal should be at the top of the rose. Wrap the next petal around the first one, positioning the thin end at the top and starting ¼ inch (6 mm) before the edge of the first petal. Each petal should be offset from the placement of the one before it. Wrap the remaining petals, pressing gently at the base to secure the petals and gently using your hands to curl them.

5 When all the petals have been added, use a paring knife to trim the excess marzipan away from the base. Let the roses dry uncovered at room temperature for about 1 hour. Use tweezers to move the roses.

6 Use right away or store in an airtight container at room temperature for up to 1 week.

Red gel-paste food coloring (page 11)

5 oz (155 g) marzipan

Confectioner's sugar for dusting

INDEX

weldonowen

415 Jackson Street, Suite 200, San Francisco, CA 94111
Telephone: 415 291 0100 Fax: 415 291 8841
www.wopublishing.com

Weldon Owen is a division of

BONNIER

WELDON OWEN INC.

CEO and President Terry Newell
VP, Sales and Marketing Amy Kaneko
Director of Finance Mark Perrigo

VP and Publisher Hannah Rahill
Executive Editor Jennifer Newens
Editor Donita Boles

Associate Creative Director Emma Boys
Senior Designer Ashley Lima

Production Director Chris Hemesath
Production Manager Michelle Duggan
Color Manager Teri Bell
Photographer Maren Caruso
Author and Food Stylist Shelly Kaldunski
Prop Stylist Leigh Noe
Illustrator Salli Sue Swindell

THE ART OF THE COOKIE

Conceived and produced by Weldon Owen Inc.
Copyright © 2010 Weldon Owen Inc.

All rights reserved, including the right of reproduction
in whole or in part in any form.

Color separations by Embassy Graphics in Canada
Printed and bound by 1010 Printing, Ltd. in China
First printed in 2010
10 9 8 7 6 5 4 3

Library of Congress Cataloging-in-Publication
data is available.

ISBN-13: 978-1-61628-035-2
ISBN-10: 1-61628-035-2

ACKNOWLEDGMENTS

Weldon Owen wishes to thank the following people for their generous support in producing this book:
Copyeditor Judith Dunham; **Designer** Rachel Lopez Metzger; **Indexer** Ken DellaPenta;
Food Stylist's Assistants Ara Armstrong and Shad Eddelman; **Photographer's Assistants** Kassandra Medeiros
and Stacy Ventura; **Photographer** Emma Boys (page 9); **Proofreader** Linda Bouchard; and **Text Writer** Lauren Ladoceour.